THE POWER OF NOTHING

THE POWER OF NOTHING

The Life and Adventures of Ignacio "Idaho" Urrutia

. . . . .

Joxe Mallea-Olaetxe

IDAHO GROCERY, INC. / SUSANVILLE, CALIFORNIA 2000

Frontispiece: Ignacio Urrutia, ca. 1936–40.

to Ignacio Urrutia

CONTENTS

ILLUSTRATIONS

INTRODUCTION

This is the story of "Mr. Idaho," a Basque emigrant who arrived in the United States in 1931. He lived in Susanville, California, where everyone called him Mr. Idaho, but his real name was Ignacio Urrutia.[1] He was warm and energetic, active for a man of eighty-six. His fine features, glasses, and snow-white hair made him look like a diplomat or a professor. By his engaging gentlemanly manner, you could tell he had had years of experience dealing with the public.

Through perseverance and hard work, Urrutia became owner of a successful small business. More important, he and his wife raised a great, close-knit family. Most Basques in the American West were sheepherders, but Urrutia was not typical—though initially he, too, worked in the sheep business—and that may be an additional reason why his story should be of interest to historians and the public in general, particularly the Basques.

The reader will agree that Mr. Idaho was endowed with uncommon memory. His biography first takes us through his childhood and youth in the Basque Country and is followed by his trips to a number of countries in Europe and Africa, always bringing him closer to his goal, which was to live in the United States. But how do you do it at a time when legal immigration into the U.S. was nearly impossible for the Basques in Spain?

As he tells his story, one realizes that though strictly historical, it does not read like a mainstream historical account. One reason is that the road traveled by Urrutia is seldom traveled by most historians. He provides details so fresh and alive that only an eyewitness could have such recollections. Sometimes his contributions shed light on issues that history books often bypass or never mention, and when they do, their subject usually appears removed and devoid of real-life drama. Though the present study does not pretend to be anything more than what it is—the biography of an adventurous man—it exudes that elusive mark of authenticity to such a degree that it provides relevant reading material on immigration and ethnic and minority history in the western United States.

I will make liberal use of Urrutia's own narrative, with the goal of allowing his account to remain as direct as possible, in order to preserve that precious first-hand quality of his story from his point of view.

The information here was previously contained in audiotapes, which were recorded in the 1980s. Donald Garate was the initial interviewer, followed by Robert Olson, both of Susanville, California. At the time of drafting the manuscript in 1999, I conducted my own interviews, especially to acquire information on the post-1970 period of Urrutia's life, which was lacking. I also re-examined the data whenever I considered it necessary.[2]

I want to express my sincere and deep gratitude first to Mr. Idaho Urrutia and his family for agreeing to discuss their life and to Garate and Olson for their many hours of taping the questions and answers. Sara Vélez Mallea transcribed part of the audiotapes, and she was responsible for overseeing the final editing and production as well. *Milesker denei* (One thousand thanks to all).

THE POWER OF NOTHING

ONE

Growing Up in the Basque Mountains
· · · · ·

Ignacio Urrutia was born in Bilbao, in the Basque region of
Bizkaia, Spain, on January 31, 1913. Bilbao was and still is the
largest Basque city, a center of steel and other manufacturing,
and home to a large Spanish immigrant population.[1] In the
1990s Bilbao received much media attention with the opening of its Guggenheim Museum. Bilbao is also one of the
largest seaports in Spain. For these reasons, the language spoken in Bilbao is mostly Spanish, but Urrutia grew up in
Galdakao, Bizkaia, a small town five miles from Bilbao, which
was primarily a rural environment where mostly Euskara, the
ancient language of the Basques, was spoken.[2]

No one knows where the Basques came from to their
present-day homeland in the western Pyrenees Mountains
between France and Spain. Many experts believe that they are
descendants of the prehistoric peoples who painted wonderful
animal figures deep in the caves 10,000 to 30,000 years ago.
The Basques are the oldest human group in Western Europe;
that is, they are the "Indians" of Europe. They speak a language that is unrelated to any other on earth. They say that
the devil tried to learn Euskara, and after ten years he only
mastered two words, *bai* (yes) and *ez* (no).

Urrutia's parents were Julian San Martin and Petra Urrutia.
His father left the country and he never knew him, so naturally he was given his mother's last name. In the old days,
Basque society may have been matrilineal. We do know that
in the Middle Ages, many Basques took their names from

their mothers, even when the father was present. Petra Urrutia was born in Elgoibar, Gipuzkoa, a town directly east of Bizkaia, but it is near the border and they speak a dialect that is very similar to the Bizkaian Basque, which Urrutia learned. Urrutia remembers going with his mother just once to visit the farm where she was raised in the mountains around Elgoibar. She was a *baserritar*, a farmer woman.

Urrutia's birth certificate indicates that he was baptized in the parish of San Anton in Atxuri, which today is part of Bilbao. He does not know why his mother went to Bilbao to give birth. In 1913 the forty or so miles that separated Elgoibar from Bilbao must have seemed like a long ways off. Urrutia said dryly, "I must have been born in the hospital. I can't remember." That is Basque humor for you (how many people have any recollection of their birth, anyway?).

It is possible that Petra lived in Galdakao by then and went to Bilbao to have the baby, a normal procedure, although in the rural areas, even decades later, just about everyone was born at home. Urrutia was baptized probably on the same or following day, according to the Roman Catholic ritual.

At least since 1913 or 1914 Petra worked as a baby-sitter or housekeeper for a man named Domingo Diego, who was a traveling salesman. He sold mostly cloth from the back of his donkey. Diego was a widower with five children, the youngest of whom, a son, was nine days younger than Urrutia. In addition, Diego hired Petra as a wet nurse for his son. Petra must have been overwhelmed as she tried to be mother to six children. As a result, she had her own son sent away to a nearby farmhouse while she nursed Diego's young son. "She raised this baby with her milk . . . and I was raised with cow's milk," says Urrutia.

Growing Up in the Hills (1913–1919)

"I was raised in the mountains." says Urrutia. The recollection of mountains and hills is powerful in his memory. The mountains in the Basque Country, being very close to the Bay of Biscay and the Atlantic Ocean, are not very high, but the country is rugged and hilly with narrow green valleys. This is the land that is etched in Urrutia's mind. This is where he grew up, where he spent the first six years of his life. The farmers that raised him were friends or perhaps distant relatives of Petra Urrutia. Thus, he was to have two families during his childhood years.

The mountain hamlet where Urrutia grew up was called Bekelarri. There were three houses by that name, about an hour's walk from downtown Galdakao. One farmstead was called Minelarri, because there was a mine near it. He remembers red dirt—it was probably an iron mine—where a lot of men worked. But he did not come into contact with them, because they used Usansolo Road, which came up from the other side of the hill.

The last name of the family that raised him was Lekue-Sagarminaga (Basques always have two last names, first the father's and then the mother's). He called Mr. Lekue *aitita* (grandfather). Fermina Sagarminaga, the *etxekoandra* (lady of the house), became de facto his *ama* (mother) and *amuma* (grandmother), to the point that for six years he assumed they were his family. They had two sons and two daughters of their own, all of whom were over seventeen years old and had jobs in nearby factories.

In 1913 Bekelarri was a typical Basque rural setting (except for the mine). Urrutia's recollections include green meadows and big (for Basque Country standards) fields, lots of fruit trees, and cows: "You go into the orchard and eat your apples and the figs." Whenever the cows were nearby and he wanted a quick snack, he would get under his favorite cow and drink her milk by squirting it right out of her udder. Cows were very good and gentle with children, he says.

He spent a lot of time with Grandpa, who was doing much of the farm work. Urrutia helped as much as a little boy of his age could. Sometimes he and Grandpa went up to their pine forest to do some work. Urrutia remembers that they dug holes to make a bed of pine needles and then took a siesta. "Him and I. You know, he was with me all the time, my Grandpa," he says. His name was Juan Beniño Lekue.

All the farmers in Bekelarri—and most in Bizkaia—had at least one donkey (*asto*), a sure-footed animal ideal for carrying light loads on steep terrain, such as groceries from the store in town. Donkeys don't get lost, not even in the darkest nights. Grown-ups seldom rode a donkey; they walked with it.

Every Basque farm raises cows, mostly milk cows, which were milked twice a day. Every cow had its own name, but Urrutia does not remember any names. The Lekue-Sagarminagas had six cows and about as many calves. For breeding purposes, every farming locality had a few special bulls where the neighbors' cows were taken for a visit. But Urrutia knows these things from later years. He was unaware of them when he lived in Bekelarri. The cows doubled as draft animals as well and pulled the steel plow or the cart with wooden wheels reinforced with an iron band.

Whenever the fields were plowed, young Urrutia walked ahead of the cows, guiding them in order to keep the furrows straight. This job is called *ittaurren* in Bizkaia. The man holding onto the plow used an *akulu,* a five-foot-long stick with a short nail point with which to spur the cows.

Timber was an important part of farming in Bekelarri. Many farms in Bizkaia were part tree farms. Pines, locally called "maritime," were grown almost exclusively. As soon as timber was harvested, seedlings were replanted and kept weed free. Trees were cut with two-man saws and transported on carts pulled by oxen. In Bekelarri the farmers did not engage in logging, which was left to workers employed by the local sawmill where the logs were processed.

Most of the food that the family needed was raised right

on the farm: dry beans, string beans, potatoes, corn, wheat, eggs, and all kinds of fruit. Wheat was harvested by hand with a sickle—a back-breaking job—and threshed by women in the attic by striking it against flat stones, which were kept there for the following harvest. A group of women with kerchiefs over their heads would line up and grab an *azabu* (a bunch of tied-up wheat stalks) and hit it against the stones until all the grain came loose. Then the grain was sieved in round hand sieves and stored in *kaxak* (large deep trunks made of hardwood, which were decorated with Basque motifs hand-carved into the wood). They also grew *naboak*[3] (stock beets) and *arto* (corn). Corn ears were hung in the attic to dry.

Like most other farmers, the Lekue-Sagarminagas butchered their own beef and pork, but meat was a small part of their diet. The corn and the wheat were taken to the local water mill to be ground into flour. Every so often, as needed, a sack of the grain would be loaded on the donkey and taken to the mill, where it was exchanged for flour already ground and ready for cooking. Though the farmers did not necessarily consume their own grain, they knew, however, that it was locally grown.

The Lekue-Sagarminaga *baserri* (farmstead) was a big three-story stone house, typical of the Basque Country. A wall divided the two main components or sections: the stable and the barn on one side and the home for human habitation on the other. The latter contained an upstairs for sleeping quarters and a downstairs for the living room and the kitchen area. They also had a large *sala* upstairs, a formal chamber that was rarely used. For that reason, they converted it into a bedroom for their two daughters. Urrutia had his own bedroom. The fireplace was in the kitchen. Most cooking was done in an open fireplace, but they also had a brick oven with tin on the top. The *laratz* (a heavy hook hanging down from the chimney) with adjustable height served to hold the big *kalderea* (cauldron) in place over the fire.

Ogi (bread), the main staple, was baked regularly every week or ten days in the outdoor oven, which typically was made with brick or stone, but as Urrutia recalls, the one in Bekelarri was made of mud and stone. "Every house has an oven. Farmers do not go to town to buy bread," he says. The ovens were round or oval for a more even distribution of the heat. The coals were pushed against the wall, and the loaves of bread were placed within the circle with a *para,* a huge steel spatula with a long wooden handle, big enough to hold one sheepherder-type loaf of bread. If one made a good fire and the oven was good and hot, the bread baked to a golden-brown color with a thick crust.

Other staples were *artogie,* as Urrutia remembers, which means corn bread and was baked in the oven. It comes out golden-red in color. "Talk about flavor," he says. "You eat a piece of that and you don't have to eat anything else." *Talo* were fresh corn tortillas, lightly toasted on top of the iron stove or in a large flat skillet with a long handle over an open fire. Typically, supper might consist of a big bowl of freshly toasted hot *talo* with milk, followed by some baked apples, pears, or roasted chestnuts, depending on the season. With *esne* (milk) and *arroza* (rice), they made a popular dessert. "That was the best rice pudding. Every time they cooked it, boy, you see me in there," Urrutia says with a grin. Rice is not grown in the Basque Country.

The only items that the Lekue-Sagarminagas purchased in town were sugar and coffee and, occasionally, needles and thread. The Lekue-Sagarminagas did not sell produce. Stock was most of what they had. Theirs was subsistence farming, and any additional items they needed to purchase in town were transported on the donkey.

The kitchen was the center of the home life. There were hams, *txorizo*[4] (Basque sausage), and bacon hung to smoke from the kitchen ceiling. "And you just put that in your frying pan, a little bit, and put it with the flour tortillas . . . and that's living," Urrutia says.

Normally, seven to eight people gathered at the table, which was round. The food—beans or whatever—was placed at the center in a big pot or container, and everyone helped himself or herself with a spoon. There were no individual plates in Bekelarri during Urrutia's childhood. "It was healthy living," Urrutia muses. But health problems were not totally lacking, as he still remembers that one of the Lekue boys developed *zizare* (tapeworms), which scared the hell out of Urrutia. He says it was because they drank water from places that had frogs, snakes, and all kinds of critters.

They did not have indoor plumbing in Bekelarri. The two other houses in the mountain hamlet had their own springs, but for their drinking water the Lekue-Sagarminagas went to a little canyon below where two hills came together. There was a developed spring in there with a pipe attached where people went with their water buckets. Such places usually have a name, but the one in Bekelarri was simply called *iturri,* a generic term for spring. Young Urrutia carried water lots of times, which was sort of scary because he had to fight the snakes that slithered around the area. "I didn't like to see those animals down there. I always had a stick with me. I couldn't stand the snakes," he says. Rainwater off the farmstead roof was collected in an *aska* (trough) for the stock. The domestic animals were often turned loose within a fenced area that included a little creek, and that's where they watered.

Little Urrutia did not have too many playmates around. On Sundays he might walk up to another farmstead, located even higher on the mountain, where he had a friend. The two kids devised their own games—they would play with worms, the kind that live in pine-tree holes and bite. There was not much else to do. For the first six years of his life, Bekelarri was his world. The little boy spent hours by the fireplace in the kitchen, sometimes crying, and then at night he would go upstairs to his room to sleep alone.

He never went to Galdakao, where his real mother lived. He never saw her. For all he knew, the Lekue-Sagarminagas were his family. It seems that whenever they went to town to shop at the store where his mother lived and worked, Fermina Sagarminaga let Petra know how little "Iñixio" (Basque for Ignacio) was doing at the farm. But then, one day, the world began to change for him. His grandparents, his mother's parents, who lived in Elgoibar, hopped on the train to Galdakao and hiked up to Bekelarri for a Sunday visit with their grandson. He remembers only one such visit, and he doesn't remember their names, except that they were *aitita* (grandfather) and *amuma* (grandmother). That is when he found out who his real grandparents were. "I was getting on a different atmosphere," Urrutia says.

His grandparents brought with them a sack with "a whole bunch of money," and when he saw it he asked, "What's that?" It was, of course, the payment for his room and board. The grandparents did not stay very long. They walked down to the train station on the same day, leaving the six-year-old Urrutia wondering and reflecting.

Soon after, a young man from Galdakao showed up in Bekelarri. He was Fernando Diego, his stepbrother, who was about thirteen years old. Urrutia was told that he had to go with him, because it was time to start primary school. He felt confused, scared, and he cried, but Fernando carried him on his shoulders clear down the mountains. Urrutia was rather terrified because he had never seen this guy.

It was quite a trip. Fernando spoke only Spanish, and Urrutia spoke only Basque. It was getting dark, and after an hour's time they reached the bridge over the Ibaizabal River.[5] Urrutia had never been on a bridge before, and fright overtook him. He remembers it well. Near the bridge there was an acid factory that smelled terrible. Shortly afterward, they arrived in Galdakao and walked into the house that was to be his home for the next eleven years. There he met his mother.

To this day, Urrutia does not know why his mother sent him away to be raised by the Lekue-Sagarminagas. His guess is that when she married Domingo Diego, his stepfather probably didn't want him. Petra Urrutia was saddled with two babies of the same age, and Mr. Diego convinced her to nurse his son (whose mother had recently died) rather than hers. But the truth will never be known. "I never asked my mother a question like that," Urrutia confessed. Old Country Basques are not fond of discussing such things. No one is, for that matter.

TWO

The New Family in Town

· · · · ·

For centuries, there have been two Basque societies, the urban and the rural. The former were *kaletarak* (literally, street people, that is, those living in town) and the latter *baserritarak* (rural people). In the 1990s, 85 percent of the Basques were urban, but during Urrutia's childhood it used to be the other way around. Historically, there was considerable antagonism between these two social classes, who had very different lifestyles. Furthermore, the *baserritarak* spoke only Basque, as the Spanish and French languages did not venture very far from the urban centers. Depending on which side of the Pyrenees Mountains the Basques lived, administration and official business were conducted in Spanish or French, and for that reason many people in the urban areas were bilingual.

Urrutia's own statements make this divisive issue very clear. He described how at age six his life became immersed in a totally different environment: strange new home, strange faces, and strange people speaking a strange language. With typical *baserritar* modesty, he camouflages the cultural shock under a disguise, "At that age, I was just kind of bashful." Urrutia describes his impressions of that first day in town:

> I remember the first night I came into the house. We sat down to eat and they put a big steak on my plate, and I didn't know what it was and left it right there. Because in the hills where I was raised, the only thing

we ate was beans, potatoes, and the vegetables raised out of the garden, [which] had a little pork in it. We all sit at the table with one dish, and everybody served himself with the spoons and just reach to the middle of the table and eat. So when I got in town and they put me a big plate, a big steak, and I [thought] what's this? I looked at everybody in the kitchen, they were looking at me because they did not recognize me . . . , and pretty soon I got used to it and I said to myself, "Well, this is something new in here, a change for me."

Perhaps to relieve the traumatic changes that had been brought to bear upon her son, on certain Sundays Petra Urrutia encouraged him to go back up and visit the Lekue-Sagarminagas. She gave him a snack for the road, a large piece of chocolate and a big chunk of bread. Young Urrutia loved to return to the hills, but sometimes he was disappointed because he found nobody home. On some Sundays, the Lekue-Sagarminagas went to town, or to a nearby hamlet, to the *erromeria* (country fiesta). Dancing has always been the favorite pastime for Basque peasants. Whenever Urrutia returned to Bekelarri, he always went by himself. He would cross the bridge over the Ibaizabal River and climb the mountains. He spent most of the day up there in Bekelarri, but his mother wanted him back before dark. Basques are rather superstitious, and they don't believe in being out at night, especially in the forest. It is clear that Urrutia has fond memories of the Lekue-Sagarminagas.

. . . . .

All of a sudden, young Urrutia found himself surrounded by five stepbrothers and sisters. The oldest, Manuel Diego, emigrated to Mexico. Next in line were his stepsisters, Maria and Jesusa, followed by the youngest two brothers, Fernando and Josemari Diego, who was the same age as

Urrutia. Legally, they all shared one mother, but they were not blood kin. All of these stepbrothers and stepsisters were dead by the 1990s.

Domingo Diego and Petra Urrutia had five more children: Maria Carmen, Manolita, Encarna, Lolita, and Jesus. They were true half-brothers and sisters to Urrutia, all younger than he.

He is not sure exactly when his mother married Diego, probably in 1918. She had been working in his business as a clerk for about six years before they got married.

There is not much information on the interpersonal relationships with his mother or with his stepfamily during his first few years in Galdakao, and it is quite understandable. The language in his new home was Spanish, because the Diegos were from outside Bizkaia, from Cantabria,[1] and did not speak Basque. Urrutia communicated in Euskara with his mother and most of the people in town, who normally spoke Basque.[2] Domingo Diego treated Urrutia well. On Sundays Urrutia remembers taking the wagon and going with Domingo peddling cloth from house to house.

Learning Spanish

School was the main concern and a big headache for young Urrutia. He says that he was preoccupied because all he spoke was Basque, and instruction was entirely in Spanish: "I was confused, completely lost." He was not alone. At the time, the overwhelming majority of rural Basques in Bizkaia were mostly monolingual and did not speak Spanish, at least not until after the 1950s, when Franco's systematic extermination of the Basque culture had made some inroads even into the farmstead areas.[3]

Urrutia spoke with his mother and complained and cried about school, but she would say, "Son, in here school is in Spanish and you have to learn." Mercilessly, the teacher pinched his arm because he couldn't say the ABC's in Spanish.

He had big welts on his arms. He cried, but the teacher did not care, and he was forced to learn Spanish. It took him a while, but little by little he was getting it, and then a funny thing happened. "I left my Basque to one side," Urrutia says. This was the time of General Primo de Rivera's dictatorship (1923–1930), when the central government in Madrid began attacking Basque culture in earnest.

The School Years (1919–1927)

Instruction in Galdakao's public schools went from 9 A.M. to noon and from 1 P.M. to 4:30 P.M. School opening was announced by a bell. Children from the farmsteads had to walk to school, sometimes for an hour, one way, as there were no school buses back then. Not that schools were totally lacking in outlying hamlets, for the government of Bizkaia had already built *Auzo-Eskolak* (country schools) in remote areas.

From noon to 1 P.M. it was lunchtime, and Urrutia walked home, which was five minutes away. By the time he arrived, lunch was served. The menu ordinarily consisted of soup, beans or potatoes, some kind of a stew—made with meat or fish—and dessert, usually fruit. Students from faraway farmsteads brought their own lunch. After the meal, grown-ups took a siesta, but the children had to return to school.

The schoolrooms in Galdakao were housed in one large building, but boys and girls were segregated. Boys had male teachers, and girls had female ones.[4] There were four grades, and each had its own room, with a photograph of the king. There were also special rooms for certain subjects, such as geography. A student stayed in the same room until all the material was covered. After that, he/she was transferred to the next higher grade in another room.

The teachers in Galdakao had their jobs cut out for them, because, as Urrutia remembers, there were seventy students in each class and only one teacher. The students sat at wooden desks that accommodated two or three pupils. Under the desk cover there was room for books and other materials. A little hole for the ink container was positioned on the desktop in a corner, away from the hinged cover. Each classroom contained one or two large blackboards, and they used chalk to write on them.

The teacher's large desk, located up front and facing the pupils, was elevated for a commanding view of the classroom. Urrutia was often called upon to prove that he had studied. He may have been singled out because at a tender age he had already started to help out in the family business, and the teacher wanted to make sure that he did not neglect his school work. The history of Spain and sacred history (the Bible and religion) were two of the subjects he remembers.

The teacher sent Urrutia to the blackboard, where he had to do math problems while the whole class watched. "I always received good grades," says Urrutia. According to his recollections, everybody studied pretty hard back then, specially him. Sometimes past midnight, when everyone in the family slept, he was still studying and preparing his lessons for the following day.

Discipline was rigorous. If you didn't study, misbehaved, or made too much noise, you could get a whipping. As punishment, there was a big column in the center of a hallway where the unfortunate student was directed to stand while the teacher beat him with a double-leather strap. Meanwhile, he had better not move, or the whipping might continue longer and harder. The column was a symbol of disgrace and was feared by all. One day, Urrutia called a classmate "sissy," and the teacher ordered him to stand next to the column for two hours for two days after school. He protested because he had to work, but the teacher did not budge. That was the only time he got in trouble.

It was a different story with his stepbrother, Josemari. Every afternoon, just before leaving, the pupils sang patriotic songs in the hallway hailing the government, the king, the

Dr. Gandasegui's school with seventy-five students in Galdakao, Bizkaia. Ignacio Urrutia (seventh from left in front row) and his stepbrother, Josemari Diego (extreme right in second row), 1919.

flag, and the armed forces. While singing one day, Josemari apparently raised his voice a bit too loudly, and the teacher—a substitute one—slapped him so hard that he was knocked down. Josemari left school crying and went across the plaza directly to one of the family warehouses, where his older brother, Fernando, was working. After listening to his brother's story, Fernando waited until the substitute teacher came out of the school building. When he did, he rushed over and, in retaliation, he hit him. But that was not the end of it, for some time later Fernando was taken to court and fined about forty *pesetas*, which was a lot of money back then. But after that, his brother was not hit anymore, at least not by that substitute teacher.

Classroom discipline was much more severe if a student was involved in a fight. Then you were taken into the bathroom, ordered to lower your pants, and struck on your behind with a stick.[5]

Students did not have to buy any books. Urrutia says that they were given paper and all the necessary materials, but they could not take books home. After you finished studying a book, someone else inherited it. He remembers studying a lot of geography. They drew maps of all the nations of the world in different colors. When they were ready to graduate from that particular class, these maps and other class work were put on display, and all the families of the students visited the classroom to review them. For the students, that was like the graduation ceremony.

When Urrutia was about ten years old, he had already made up his mind that he wanted to go to the United States. But at the time it was pure dream, too far down the road. His mother told him that her sister lived in Boise, Idaho. In fact, they received several letters from her, but his mother never told him to leave the country and go to Idaho or any such thing. Because of this aspiration, he was especially interested in drawing and studying the map of the United States.

Typically, primary education lasted until the teenagers began working permanently. In Urrutia's case, it ended when he was fourteen years old. During the period in question, most rural boys and girls did not attend school regularly, because farm chores took precedence over education. (The same thing was happening in the rural areas of the United States.)

The Family Business (1919–1931)

Immediately after Urrutia was brought down from the hills, his life became a lot more hectic. He not only had to apply himself to school intensely in order to keep up, but in addition, after school he was given chores to do in the business his stepfather owned in Galdakao. Gone were the siestas under the pine trees with Grandpa Lekue in Bekelarri.

By then, Domingo Diego had graduated to greater things than being a mere *kinkileru* (door-to-door salesman of cloth, needles, and such).[6] He had become a businessman operating from several warehouses in Galdakao. He ran a considerable mercantile business, the only one of its kind in town. In addition, Petra Urrutia[7] ran her own team of seamstresses and a grocery store. The name of the business was Comercio de Diego, and it comprised three warehouses, two of which were located downtown, on and near the town's plaza.

Mr. Diego traveled in order to buy merchandise that he believed he could resell at a profit. Basically, that was the extent of the enterprise: buy wholesale and sell retail. In addition to the regular merchandise Diego stocked, one could order just about anything else. Diego was gone part of the time, and Petra and his son Fernando were left in charge. Petra, too, traveled, usually to Gipuzkoa by train, to procure the necessary merchandise and materials for her seamstresses. She also bought the shoes she offered at the store.

Of the three warehouses they operated, one stored coal and charcoal and was located under the city government building, facing the plaza. The one where potatoes, straw, and alfalfa were kept was situated on the main highway out toward the town of Zornotza/Amorebietia. The third warehouse was five minutes away from the plaza, on the hill near the old church of Andra Mari.

The warehouse on the hill was the center of their business, as well as of family activities. It was a four-story building, on the ground floor of which Petra Urrutia ran a combination grocery and mercantile store, which accommodated two additional rooms in the back: a bedroom for Petra and Domingo and the kitchen where the family ate. The other space on the ground floor was occupied by a pharmacy. The rest of the upstairs floors were occupied by tenants, where Iñixio Ondabeitia, the landlord, the pharmacist, and others lived.

Adjacent to this building was a two-story edifice consisting of a warehouse downstairs and sleeping quarters upstairs. Diego stored *pentzu* (stock feed), flour, and other grains on the ground floor. Upstairs the children had their bedrooms, including Urrutia and a hired girl. Petra's seamstresses occupied the remaining space upstairs. This two-story building was bombed by Italians during the Civil War in 1937, and that ended the hiring of the seamstresses, though Petra continued to provide sewing services out of the grocery store.

Early Taste of Hard Life

It was strictly a family business, though later they hired a couple of outside people as well. It appears that Mr. Diego ran a tight ship, at least from Urrutia's point of view. He was just seven years old, yet every day, as soon as he left school, instead of going out to play in the plaza with his friends, Urrutia had to proceed to the nearby warehouse to fill sacks, deliver merchandise to the customers, or help out in the store doing whatever he was told to do. In fact, he even worked in the morning, before going to school at 9 A.M. He had no life, as we say today.

As soon as he was judged able to work, Urrutia's day began at 5 A.M. He slept in the same room as his stepbrothers Fernando and Josemari. In fact, the latter shared the bed with him. They were the same age and they attended the same school until they became fourteen, but only Urrutia got up at 5 A.M.

> It was my routine, just like I do today here [in the United States], but here nobody calls me to get up. That is the only difference [he says with a smile].
>
> In those days [during the teenage years] I was tired, working all the time, lifting, you know, the two-hundred-pound sacks to the wagon. When you go home you just feel like lying down. So in the morning I guess he [the stepfather] probably called me a couple of times, and then the second time I probably got up and got my clothes and went up to the barn. The barn was in the same building, so I didn't have to go far. I fed grain to the horse and the donkey and cleaned them up with a

brush. Then I just put the harness on and they were ready [to go out on deliveries].

After that, Urrutia went to the warehouse to get the sacks ready for delivery. He separated the ones that had holes from the good ones. After a while, Fernando, who was about seven years older, showed up. One of them held the sacks open and the other filled them with whatever the customers wanted. Urrutia and Fernando carried the business load. Josemari did not do much of this kind of work. He was thin and sickly. He had nice clean hands, like intellectuals or the high class, Urrutia says.

> He was different. He wasn't as strong as I. I don't know
> what happened. He was the weaker in the family. He
> did not have that zip like I had. I was just, go in there
> and get the sacks and load the wagon and back and forth,
> and nothing would stop me. I was strong, but he was
> different.

That may have been one reason why Josemari went to college. Yet he wasn't an outstanding student either. In fact, Urrutia had better grades than Josemari, who nevertheless went to military school and eventually became a general.

The Diego business sold great quantities of coal, which most people used for cooking. The coke arrived on ships from Great Britain to the port of Bilbao, where it was transferred into trucks or freight trains and transported to a depot in Galdakao. The Diegos had to go over with a horse-drawn wagon and haul it back to the warehouse. The loading and unloading was done all by hand, with a shovel. If dump trucks were used, the coal was dumped in front of the warehouse and then shoveled inside. It was a dusty job. But the wood charcoal, which they also sold, though lighter, was even dustier.

First Communion. Left to right: Ignacio Urrutia and his stepbrother Josemari Diego, Galdakao, Bizkaia, 1925.

Low-Tech Equipment

The main equipment owned by the Diego business was a horse, a wagon, and a donkey. The wagon was a two-wheel vehicle with a flat bed measuring about 12 × 10 feet. It could hold some thirty-five to forty bales of hay, which was sold to the farmers. It was critical that the load be balanced evenly front and back, so that all the horse had to do was pull. Of course, four wheels would have been much more comfortable for the horse but would have added weight to the wagon.

Unlike in the United States, Urrutia chuckles, the wagon did not need a license plate or anything. The horse fit between two long poles that were attached to the collar. The wagon had no seat for a rider, so whenever Urrutia was delivering the orders, he walked beside the horse's head holding the reins. On the way back to the warehouse, he rode the wagon. In town and on easy roads, the wagon was used, but only the donkey could deliver feed and other supplies to the farms in the hills. Obviously, the wise donkey prayed for an active road crew to pave as many roads as possible, but in a hilly country like Bizkaia, it just could never be fast enough.

Urrutia still remembers a scene he once witnessed of a man and his jackass pulling a big load. The man hit the jackass with a stick to keep the beast going, all along singing a Spanish rhyme:

Arre, perico,	*Come on, jackass,*
el que nació para pobre	*when destined to be poor*
nunca llegará a ser rico.	*one can never become rich.*

Urrutia took the rhyme and its meaning to heart.

After school in the afternoons, Urrutia was always busy with deliveries. He began by age eight first delivering light loads around the warehouse with the wheelbarrow. It rains a lot in Bizkaia and sometimes the iron wheel would get stuck in the mud, and Urrutia had to manage to get it unstuck. By age twelve he was doing the work of a man and going out with the horse and donkey on deliveries.

About the worst part of his routine was handling the charcoal, which was sold in one-hundred-pound sacks. He loaded the wagon with the sacks and went down the streets, and whenever a woman hollered from the window, "I want some," he shouldered the sack and hauled it upstairs four to five stories into the kitchen, where families had a little wooden box for the charcoal. Sometimes Urrutia got a tip for delivering, usually five or ten cents.

People used coal for cooking as well as for heat. The stoves were similar to the ones in the United States, made of cast iron with a removable top. People filled the firebox with coal and "you had heat for a long time," says Urrutia. It never gets too cold in that part of the Basque Country with a maritime climate.

At this point, interviewer Robert Olson asks about the danger of fires, and Urrutia replies he had never seen a house burning (it rains too much, for one thing). In fact, he added, he did not remember seeing a fire department in town. Most houses have thick rock or brick walls. They do have, however, chimney sweeps who scuff the soot off the chimney walls with a rope to which a scraper is attached. One guy on the roof does the job by pulling the rope up and down.

The Trips Back to the Mountains

It seems that Urrutia's preferred task was delivering feed to the farmers, because it gave him a chance to return to the place and environment in which he felt comfortable. He contrasts the different cultures of the *baserri* (farmstead) and the town (*kale*): "The only time I was talking Basque was when I was delivering up to the ranches where all the people talked Basque . . . , and I just kept my Basque with them. But when I went to the school I had to leave it all one sides and back on my Spanish." The Diegos were mono-lingually Spanish, though his stepfather, Domingo, spoke a little broken Basque, which he needed in the few times he went to deliver to the farmers. Francisco Cano, the hired hand from Cantabria, did not speak Basque either.

Much of the merchandise they sold consisted of bales of alfalfa and straw, which came from Nafarroa by train. They were tied with two wires, and a donkey could carry four bales at a time. Normally, farmers bought one or two alfalfa bales each. Urrutia also delivered peat for the stock and a lot of grain, particularly horse beans. The latter had a lot of dirt mixed in and had to be screened clean before delivery.

Worse yet, the beans were infested with worms that crawled up Urrutia's legs, and he felt thoroughly disgusted. Being of tender age, he cried, but he was told he had to do the work. The horse beans were first soaked in water before feeding them to the cows, pigs, and other farm animals.

After the deliveries, the farmers usually treated him with a glass of wine, a *txorizo* (sausage), and a piece of bread. "They always treat you right," says Urrutia. He enjoyed that part, but still the days were hard and long. Sometimes it was so late that when he arrived with the feed the farmers were already in bed. He woke them up and they would say, "Gee, you sure late. Just leave it [merchandise] right there." But then a tender-hearted *etxekoandra* would say, "Come in, I want to warm up this little bit of food I have. You got to eat something, you still got another hour and a half" (before you get back home). So he would snack on potatoes with gravy or something, always with a glass of red wine. And out he went again into the darkness, rain or shine (mostly the former).

Today in the United States, we can hardly imagine sending a boy of twelve out on delivery until the wee hours. Some might respond that it was different in the 1920s, but the fact is that young Urrutia was afraid of the darkness and terrified to be out at night. The fear of darkness was cultural. In rural areas, children are taught to be afraid of *gaueko* (the beings of the night). People are "beings of the day" who are supposed to stay home once darkness falls. According to popular beliefs and legends, people who disobey these rules are punished.

No wonder that when his last deliveries were completed, Urrutia gladly clung to his donkey, who did not need to be told which road went home. He says, "Yeah, I rode it because it was dark, and I was scared coming through the bushes. You always hear stories about kidnapping and things, so I was worried all the time."[8]

Sometimes he also had the wagon and the horse to tend to when he returned to the bottom of the mountain. He would tie the donkey behind the wagon and take the animals back to the barn, unhitch them, and feed them. In spite of the snacks the farmers gave Urrutia, he was still hungry when he arrived home. Sometimes he ate supper at midnight or later, depending on the deliveries.

Doing Most of the Work

The interviewer Donald Garate was justified in asking of Urrutia if he was making all the deliveries. The answer was, "Yeah, I was doing all the work." Normally, Urrutia made about ten deliveries. Garate's next logical question was what the rest of the family members were doing. Urrutia said that some of his stepbrothers were in college and some in the army, and someone had to stay home and work. But then he added, "I wanted to go to school, too, and to the university, just like the others, but there wasn't room for all of us. Somebody had to be there [with the business to finance the college careers]. We hired another guy to work [Cano], so this guy and I were in charge of the deliveries."

It appeared that Mr. Diego hit the jackpot with Urrutia, who in typical Basque-peasant fashion was a hard worker and extremely dependable. How much did he pay him? Family members received no salary. Furthermore, Urrutia feels that he was neglected and received less attention than the rest of the family members.

From 1919 until he left Galdakao, Urrutia's life centered around work rather than around family and friends, as is the rule especially during teenage years. Everyone in the family seemed to be too busy with the business or college. Father was gone on business quite a bit, and mother not only had a large household but besides she worked in the grocery store and managed a dozen employees of her own.

Urrutia says that business was good and that the family

stores were thriving. They were not rich, but they were better off than average. "But we worked. Our policy was to work. Everybody work. Play was out," he adds. He wanted to go out and spend time with friends, but it was not allowed.

Business Details

Diego stored different goods in his three warehouses, as described earlier: hay and potatoes in one, coal in the other, and flour, grain, corn, and all the fancier stuff in the third building above which the Diego family lived. Rats from the little creek that ran nearby fed on the potatoes, and a few mice lived happily in the midst of the flour and the grains, Urrutia says. One day when he went to his mother's house, he thought he saw a chicken in the street, but it turned out to be a huge rat. In many Basque towns, some houses are built right over the creeks, so rats are never too far. In any event, the family tried not to keep excessive inventory, lest they lose too much to such critters and to spoilage, because it is very damp in Galdakao.

The goods Diego marketed came from different provinces, some from regions adjacent to the Basque Country, such as Rioja, the famed wine country. Flour and corn were shipped in. Araba and Nafarroa produced potatoes, hay, and some grain. Historically, Bizkaia and Gipuzkoa produced no surplus agricultural products, except apples, but Urrutia says that during his boyhood the farmers harvested quite a few potatoes. Diego sold eating as well as certified seed potatoes in the store. As late as the 1980s, Petra Urrutia still sold potatoes and other things in her store.

A bread factory was located close to Bilbao, and Urrutia drove the wagon there to get loads of bran. The round-trip might take six hours. Diego sold bran to the farmers, who thought it was too rough for human consumption and fed it to the cows, the calves, the pigs, and the chickens. At that time Basque farmers practiced subsistence farming, and they produced much more than they do today, including meat and milk, which were cash crops.

No store in Galdakao sold any milk, because it was brought fresh from the farms every single day of the year. Every morning, farmers from the mountains brought their milk in five-gallon cans loaded in a little wagon drawn by a jackass. The wagon might hold five or six cans belonging to different farmers living in the same hamlet. They went down the streets peddling the milk from house to house. Customers came out with their own two-liter or gallon containers. Urrutia himself was in the streets every day, and he watched these milk transactions lots of times. He also saw milk being poured down the street gutter whenever the inspector came and found that it had been *baptized* (that is, it contained too much water). As a rule, the farmers became incensed by these measures, but it was better than paying a fine.

Another commodity that was sold fresh every day was fish. Women vendors from the ports of Bilbao, Elantxobe, or Bermeo came to town with their baskets, hawking all types of fish through the streets. To this day, Basques consume a lot of fish, but some of the favorites were *legatz* (hake), *sardinak* (sardines), *bixigu* (sea bream), and others like *txipiroi* (calamari). "Every day they came in with a different type of fish. You always have a variety," recalls Urrutia.

Today in the Basque Country, meat is much more available than back then, Urrutia observes. Another change is that Galdakao used to be a town of seven thousand and now is up to fifty thousand. "The last time I was there, I didn't see anybody hauling a hundred-pound sack of coal up the stairs either," he adds with a grin. The apartment houses now are ten to fifteen stories high, and Urrutia looks at them and is glad that they didn't have them in his day. People today use propane gas for cooking, which is distributed in steel containers that are delivered to the street addresses, but the customers have to come down and take them upstairs themselves.[9]

Food and Wine Culture

In the morning, after the wagon, the animals, and the sacks were ready for delivery, the family ate breakfast, which was about 8 A.M. One of the younger sisters would come into the warehouse and announce, "Time to eat." The Diego kitchen contained hams hanging from the ceiling, and the cook cut a slice and served it with fried eggs and bread. Breakfast, unlike the noon dinner, was dispatched on the run, but they never forgot to pray before every meal—and before going to bed. Though most Basques did not have wine for breakfast, Urrutia says that they had it with every meal. The reason was that breakfast for them was more like brunch, considering that he had been up since 5 A.M.

In the Basque Country, people seldom drank any water, which was not of very good quality—"it's got a lot of seeds and stuff"—unless it came from a spring, Urrutia says. One wonders if Basque society did not suffer from water starvation. Little beer was consumed at the time, and few other prepared drinks such as colas and seltzer were in the market or consumed by the general population. The children drank milk, but normally the adults only had it for breakfast with coffee, in the *esnezopa* (warm milk with pieces of bread), or with *artozopa* (same as latter dish but with corn instead of bread). A popular song in Spanish says, "Milk for babies, water for the frogs, and wine for adults." The trick, it seems, was that the Basques got their intake of water through broth, soups, stews, and the occasional glass of water.

Most of the liquids they drank tasted like wine. Whenever he made the deliveries, Urrutia says, "The first thing they bring you was the wine." Running out of wine was a cause for emergency. Farmers kept their wine in large pig-skin containers called *zahagi*. One of the legs served as the spout, which was stopped with a cork. Another popular vessel was the *garrafoi,* a fifteen-gallon padded glass bottle.

Wine was big business, a commodity, and there were several wholesalers in each town. The Diegos drank wine from the famed Rioja region, part of which was in the Basque region of Araba. Nafarroa also produced wine, but Bizkaians favored Rioja. Bizkaia and Gipuzkoa lack sufficient sun and produced only a bit of local green wine called *txakolina*.

When river water was low, the mills in Galdakao stopped working, but those in Zornotza/Amorebieta, about five miles away, continued grinding grain. Every so often, as needed, Urrutia took a wagonload of corn or wheat to a mill there and returned with a load of flour. But before leaving town, he stopped by a wine warehouse to get the usual supply for the family. They knew him and they knew Mr. Diego, so the wholesaler had no qualms selling wine to him. The problem was hiding the *zahagi* in the middle of the flour sacks. Bizkaia was far from being a dry county, so why this behavior, the reader might ask. The reason was that sales tax was the only tax Bizkaia had at the time. Big industries, steel mills, and businesses paid no tax. So on the highway, positioned between every town, there was a tax inspector. When Urrutia passed by, the inspector came over and asked him if he was bringing any wine, and he would answer, "no," thus avoiding the tax. So the next time he went to the wine warehouse, he returned the empty *zahagi* and received a full one, and so on.

Petra Urrutia's Business

Petra Urrutia hired about a dozen women and ran a sewing business in a room above the warehouse. It was another angle of the family business. Naturally, she also sold clothing material by the yard. This was before K-Mart and the ready-made clothes we enjoy today were available. People had to first select from a catalogue the type of dress or suit they liked, then they bought the material, after which the seamstress or the tailor proceeded to take his/her measurements. A couple of weeks later, the customer came in for the first try and, if everything fit OK, the seamstress proceeded to finish the sewing. The customer returned for the second fit and final try-on, and, if satisfied, paid the bill and took the suit or dress home.

The seamstresses, some older, some younger, were full-time employees, and Petra Urrutia paid them by the day. Some worked with sewing machines—the business had five or six such machines—while others did embroidering, alterations, or whatever else the customer requested.

The Mercantile Store

The grocery store was managed by Petra and her eldest daughter. They sold "everything" in there, says Urrutia: shoes, *espartinak*[10] (slippers made with esparto), *txapelak* (berets), candles, lamps, etc. The shoes were shipped from the factory in Errenderi, Gipuzkoa. However, they did not sell farm tools like shovels and scythes and other implements, as one would have expected.

The candle business was brisk; they sold little ones and big ones and hung the small ones on nails on the wall. People came in to buy candles on Sunday mornings just before going to mass. In church there was a special place for lighting candles. "You go to church and you cannot breathe; the smoke is so thick, you cannot even see what's going on. Everybody's got their own candles burning," Urrutia says. Farmers used candles for lighting, but in town they had electricity. People used kerosene lamps, too, but the store didn't carry them.

Church chairs were another item they stocked. These

were special chairs with a seat low to the ground, which served also as a kneeler, but their backs were high and had a flat top for people to rest their arms. These chairs remained in church all the time and nobody used them but the owner, who was always a woman, the representative of the family. Her name was engraved on the armrest or printed on a label, held in place with gold thumbtacks. "They looked pretty," says Urrutia. The wood that the chairs were made of was light. The churches in the Basque Country were full of these chairs.[11]

Time Out: Playing Handball and Swimming

Urrutia worked seven days a week, but on Sunday mornings everybody went to church for mass. The church of Andra Mari dedicated to the Virgin Mary was just across the street from home. As a boy, he played handball with the priests, right against the church wall (which was forbidden in some towns). Don Mariano was the pastor, and he had four assistants: Don Prudencio, Don Tomas, and Don Emilio, who was a young priest. They all played handball with Urrutia. Don Tomas was a musician and gave piano lessons, but once in a while he would come out and say, "Come on, let's go play handball."

As a boy growing up in that church-oriented environment, he recalls being around and in-and-out of the church building almost every day, because some of his friends were altar boys. After school, the children went to a large classroom adjacent to the church building where the priests taught catechism. Sometimes the kids went to the bell tower to ring the bells. It was sort of a mysterious place up there, where big old birds made their nests. "We were scared," Urrutia says.

Occasionally, even during the week, he would sneak out for an hour or so of handball and then rush back to the warehouse. Once in a while on Sundays he also played soccer. They had sort of a secret team with uniforms and everything.

Urrutia envied his friends, particularly the ones living in town, because they had a lot more free time than he ever did.

It was during one of those precious off-duty times that he learned to swim in the Ibaizabal River. He had little choice, in fact: it was either learn to swim, or else. It happened one summer day when they were frolicking in the river, and this friend of his, a bigger guy, enticed him to swim across the river.

"Come on, you can make it," he kept saying to him.

"Halfway is as far as I can go," Urrutia replied.

"I will help you, if anything happens," the guy assured him.

"No," Urrutia resisted.

"Oh, come on, I will bet you can do it," he pressured him.

Betting is one way the Basques resolve their differences, and Urrutia finally caved in. Off into deep water the two friends went, and suddenly the younger swimmer panicked and began to go under. As Urrutia came up, in desperation, he threw his hands out to grab at anything, which turned out to be his friend's neck. He would not let go either. The boys lived some frightening moments, but in the end they made it across safely. It was one scare Urrutia never forgot. "That's when I learned to swim," he says philosophically.

Growing Up with Maids

The members of the Diego-Urrutia family could afford to buy some of the finer things, such as suits. They could afford other luxuries as well, such as maids. Two hired girls—one was seasonal—did the cooking, the laundry, and the ironing. Petra Urrutia of course was in charge of the home. She supervised the maids and their activities, especially the cooking, by specifying the menu of each day. Their stove could use either wood or coal, but normally they burned the latter. Wood was used only for special cooking.

Petra made sure that every Monday morning the maid had

readied all the clothes for the week and they were sitting right on top of everyone's bed. The washing was done down the creek about a quarter mile away. Urrutia put the wash into buckets, loaded them on the wagon, and drove it to the river. The hired girl did the washing on some special flat rocks, using a regular bar of soap and a brush. Urrutia remembers the creek water being very clean. It took the girl most of the day to do the wash, because there were fifteen of them in the family, counting the maids. At about 4 or 5 P.M. Urrutia took his wagon down to the creek again and picked up the clean laundry, which was hung on the clothesline in back of the warehouse, that is, behind the horse's and donkey's stable. They strung the lines from one fruit tree to another. After the clothes dried—not a simple matter in the humid climate of Bizkaia—the other maid ironed them. Once a year, these maids were paid a salary of one hundred *pesetas* (room and board was included).

Feeling Discriminated Against

When the Diego boys went to college or the university, Urrutia had to assume additional responsibilities and to take on even a greater share of the work load. Of course, the family business paid for all the college expenses. Most of the children went to Bilbao or to Deusto, which is across the river from Bilbao.[12] Diego's oldest son, Manuel, went to college in the city of Santander, after which he sailed to Mexico to join his uncle's business. Before leaving, he came to Galdakao to say good-bye, and that is when Urrutia first met him.

One reason why Urrutia worked so hard was that he did not fit very well with the Diego family. Some nights he arrived home late and dead tired, but his stepbrother Fernando was not in bed. He had volunteered into the army for six months, which in effect required a payment, a purchase, in order to avoid being drafted later and going through regular military service like everyone else. Fernando was serving in

Bilbao, where he had a girlfriend. As a volunteer, he had a lot of freedom and came home often. At night, unbeknownst to all but his brothers, he would jump out of the window, go down the hill, and take the streetcar to Bilbao to see his girlfriend. He would not return until 3 or 4 A.M., and he probably came back in a taxi because the streetcars did not run that late. Petra knew about it but told her son to keep it quiet. The escapades didn't trouble Urrutia, but the fact that Fernando was managing the business money did. "I think he was throwing away quite a bit [of money]. Of course, the business was good, but a lot of money was going in the drain, too," he says. And that hurt, because he was the only one who day after day had to get up at 5 A.M., feed and clean the horse and the donkey, put the harness on them, and make ready for another long day. The loading took place at the warehouse on the plaza, across from the school, or at the one on the hill by the church, depending on the orders to be filled on that particular day.

When the boys went to college, the family hired Francisco Cano to help Urrutia. He was about two years older than Urrutia, and he liked to sing Spanish songs. He was an all-around helper, but he could not make deliveries into the farming areas because he did not speak Basque.

The Diego boys were given a college education, but no such luck for Urrutia. Is it any surprise that he felt neglected? "I didn't see any love between the brothers. Just slave, do this and do that, and just keep on doing it," he recalls. Worse yet, he was occasionally mistreated by Fernando. Domingo, the stepfather, on the other hand, treated him well. It appears that he was a jolly man, liked to play cards and spend time at the bar.

Meanwhile, orders and deliveries piled up on Urrutia's shoulders, and he sometimes complained that he couldn't do it all. "Did they think it was a joke that day after day, he [I] was out working late and returning home sometime around midnight?" Urrutia says. That is when Fernando got rough with him, slapping and kicking him sometimes. Some folks who saw it told him that such treatment was not fair, but he could only respond that he had plans and he would stay until the time came for him to leave. Fortunately, Urrutia had a good relationship with his mother. "She knew the situation, but she couldn't do anything," he says. She tried to offer him support.

In addition, like many other Basques, he had a bit of adventurer in his blood and he believed that the world offered a young man excitement and exploits. He was eager to experiment, he knew he had the energy, and he was ambitious. But meanwhile, things in the business were not improving. On the contrary.

Urrutia was about fifteen when Fernando went into the army, and even more of the work load was thrown upon his shoulders—business management and bookkeeping. Josemari perhaps could help, but he was away in college. It appears that Mr. Diego had no training as a bookkeeper, so Urrutia started attending night class to study accounting, two hours every night. These were private classes paid for by his mother. He studied hard, and eventually he was taking care of not only the deliveries but the books as well.

Urrutia took an interest in bookkeeping. All the sales were charged in Galdakao. He had a great big book with the names of the customers and the orders he had delivered to each one. At the end of six months, or whenever they came in to pay, he added up the bill and then he marked PAID. After that, he started another page with the customer's name on top. He managed the books of the business for more than two years.

THREE

Life at Sea: 1931–1932

. . . . .

For years, Urrutia was tired of working long hard hours. Sometimes it was 1:00 A.M. when he finally collapsed to sleep on the bed. He would complain to his mother, and she tried to console him, "Son, this is how life is. We have to work, etc." But he was not buying it. In spite of the long hours he worked, Urrutia received no wages whatsoever. Just some clothes and room and board. Even on Sundays, when it is customary to go out with friends and have a drink or two, he did not have any money, though occasionally he managed to steal away and do it. (Although Urrutia was still a teenager, he had been working as an adult, and culturally he was considered a grownup.)

After 1927 he was no longer in school, but bookkeeping kept him up at night. "I was getting tired, working every day, even Sundays, from morning till night, and there was no time for play, everything was work. I had all I could take, so when I was seventeen, I already had my plans to get in the merchant marine," he recalls.

The Big Move

The merchant ship was his ticket to the United States. He had been corresponding with his aunt and cousins in Boise, and they encouraged him to come over. He began making inquiries, but kept quiet about it. One day he went to Bilbao to the office of a merchant marine company, where he was told to enlist first in the Spanish navy. Without missing a beat, he

[35]

went into the naval office and enlisted. He returned to the merchant marine office and was immediately offered a job on a ship sailing out of Great Britain. That was all it took.

The Diegos did not know about his plans, but even if they had, they would not have stopped him from leaving; they could not, even if they tried. Only Petra Urrutia knew about his plans. She told him, "Son, I wish you didn't leave because Jesus [his half-brother] is too young yet [he was one and a half years old], he's just a baby, and I wish you would stay until he grows up."

"Mother, he will grow up, like I did. We got hired help here, and the [hired] girl will take care of things. Mother, my mind is already made up," Urrutia replied.

One early morning in April 1931, Urrutia left while his mother was in church, as was her routine. Jesus was still asleep. It was about 6 A.M., and he left without saying good-bye to his mother, because he knew she would hurt even more.

The only money he had when he left Galdakao was that which his uncle Martin Urrutia of Elgoibar, the mother's brother, gave him. He had spent some years herding sheep for Andrew Little in Idaho and had returned home to set up a clothing business. When Urrutia went to Gipuzkoa to say good-bye to his uncle—he was the only close family member—he gave him $300, or about 1,500 *pesetas.* It was quite a bit of money, and Urrutia did not think he needed it, but his uncle reminded him that he could be without a job and in need of money for food, hotels, etc.

Urrutia took the hired girl along to help carry the suitcase. It was small and he could have carried it himself, but, he says, "In those days I was a businessman, part of a higher class, so she carried the suitcase and I carried the raincoat on my arm." As he walked, he kept looking at the windows and saw all the women looking through the window while they were cooking breakfast for their husbands and sons who worked in the local factories. They started work at 7 A.M., and he wanted to

*Ignacio Urrutia (right) and an
unidentified man, ca. early 1930s.*

be gone before that. He waved at a few people as he walked down the street. When they arrived at the streetcar, he told the hired girl not to say anything if somebody asked for him. But she could not keep a secret for very long, Urrutia says.

I Want to Go Home!

Thirty minutes later he was in Bilbao, and the docks were a short walk away. At the merchant marine office, he was told which ship was his and was given a signal to identify himself to the sailors. So he stood at the dock and waved his coat. Pretty soon, he saw a small boat coming from the ship toward him, and the man rowing it asked him to identify himself, after which he was told to jump into the boat. For seventeen years he had been on dry land and now, seeing nothing but water around him, Urrutia was not so sure about his decision. But he was a man who would not look back. It was April 21, 1931.

On the big ship he soon met another man from Natxitua, Bizkaia, two to three years younger than himself. He was from the mountains, *baserritarra,* a peasant farmer. He looked very young, and he and Urrutia had been hired to work as *marmitones,* or kitchen helpers, on ships sailing the British coast. Urrutia had just turned eighteen. They were passengers from Bilbao to England on this steamship that had a steel hull but was dirty and old. The company was from Bilbao, but Urrutia does not remember which one it was—Aznar, Ibarra, or some other.

A few minutes after the ship left the calm waters of the estuary and its bow faced the open ocean, the two young men became seasick. They had never experienced that feeling of queasiness before. They were crying, but there was no one around to help.

"I want to go home," the man from Natxitua bellowed.

"Me, too," Urrutia agreed.

It was pretty disgusting, throwing up and everything. At that moment, they saw another ship sailing in the opposite direction, and Urrutia said, "Look, that ship is going to Bilbao. Shall we jump?"

The man from Natxitua, not quite as courageous, responded, "No, no. How are we going to swim clear over there? We cannot jump."

The two prospective sailors, even before they had tried their new occupations, were already fed up with ships. They were land-based animals, and they did not like the oceanic environment at all.

Later that day, they arrived in Barrydock, England, and by then they had almost forgotten about their seasickness. The vessel dropped anchor near a cargo ship that looked identical —another steamship belonging to the same company. After transferring over to the other ship, Urrutia was informed of his duties. As a kitchen helper, his job consisted of doing the dishes, peeling potatoes, and stuff like that. He did not have to cook, but when the cook went to sleep he took care of whatever was on the stove.

On the First Merchant Ship

On his first sea voyage out of England, the ship was carrying coal, and they sailed south on the Atlantic Ocean. They arrived in Lisbon, and after docking, the cook sent Urrutia into town to buy some fresh fish. He had never been in Lisbon and did not speak Portuguese, but the cook sent him off after giving him directions. He found the fish market and purchased some twenty-three pounds of fish fillets, and then he waited a few minutes for the streetcar. When it arrived, he hopped on and placed the box full of fish nearby on the floor.

It was about a ten-minute ride to the port, but when the ticket inspector showed up and saw the fish—actually, he smelled it—he told Urrutia that the car was for people, not for fish. He then positioned himself to kick the box out into the street, but Urrutia, who was young and strong, quickly grabbed it and was prepared not to let it go. Back and forth they spent some tense yet funny moments, the older and bigger man kicking at the box, and the younger and smaller hanging on to it until he saw the docks. Presto, he pulled the cord to signal the car to stop. "Now you can kick all you want," he muttered to the inspector as he jumped off the car with his fish.

From Lisbon they headed for North Africa and then to the island of Malta. The voyage lasted about a week, during which time the man shoveling coal took ill, and Urrutia was assigned to take over his job. The engines were fed coal through nine holes or fireboxes, and it was Urrutia's job to furnish the "firemen" with coal from the storage room. There were two pipes leading down into the engine room, and Urrutia just shoveled the coal down the pipes.

The cargo, that is, the coal, was unloaded in baskets, mostly by women with long dresses, and Urrutia was amazed how they were able to balance the weight as they walked between the ship and the docks. It took a month to unload the coal. In the meantime, since the ship was anchored, Urrutia returned to his original job in the kitchen.

From Malta they proceeded to Huelva, southern Spain, to load minerals. Urrutia had been at sea for about three months when he found out that he was working on the wrong ship. He heard a guy say, "No, these ships don't go to America [United States]." That was all he needed to hear. He was not interested in working on a ship that would not take him to the USA.

In Huelva, he went to see the captain and told him that he wanted to quit, because he did not like working there. Of course, he could not give him the real motive for quitting. The captain recommended that he stay with the ship. "What are you going to do? Where are you going to get a job? So many people looking for one. . . ."

"Well, I am just going to take a chance," he answered. Urrutia had given about four hundred *pesetas* to one of the officers for safekeeping, and after getting his money back he took off. Since he had his earnings, the first thing he did was to cable his uncle Martin Urrutia the three hundred dollars he had given to him.

Looking for Another Ship

He met a fellow from Valladolid, Castile. He, too, was leaving the ship and going home. He told him that he would never find a ship that went to the USA in Huelva. Urrutia took his advice and bought a train ticket to Seville, the largest city in Andalusia, which is situated on a river, but inland. More bad news awaited him there: he counted two hundred people waiting in line in the employment office. He stayed three to four days in Seville, enjoying the orange trees and the beautiful churches. He worried that his money was running short, though. He could call home or his uncle in Elgoibar, and they would have sent him the money without a problem, but he wanted to do it his way. He hopped on a train to Valencia, where he purchased a third-class ticket on a passenger ship to Barcelona. Some four hours later, he arrived in the Catalonian city.

In port Urrutia recalls an incident that he witnessed. He noticed a number of ships, and someone told him that they were full of prisoners. There had been a little revolution when King Alfonso XIII of Spain left the country (in 1931), and these individuals, his supporters, had been caught and were being held in Barcelona.

When his ship docked, Urrutia went to Chinatown, where the streets were dark and made him a bit apprehensive. But they had hotels and places where ship companies recruited sailors. He took a room in one, and he signed up for a job. Of course, money talked then as loudly as it does now, and those who could afford to slip a tip to the hotel owner were likely to get jobs in a hurry. He saw a lot of idle men, and he asked one of them, "What are the chances of getting a job on a ship?"

The man looked at him and said, "Job on the ship? You should be home. Where are you from?"

"I am from Bizkaia, Bilbao."

"What are [you] doing in here?"

"I'm just looking for a job in a ship."

"You'd better go home, you little snot.[1] How old are you?" the man asked.

"I am eighteen."

"Eighteen? Look at all the guys around you, forty, fifty, fifty-five-year-olds. They cannot get a job on the ship."

"Well, I am not leaving."

"You got a room?" the man asked.

"Yeah, I got a room, way up in the top of the building," Urrutia told him.

It was a little cubbyhole, really, with a little bed and no

lights. "I was scared to sleep in that place. Peeking through the keyhole, I watched people come and go, and I worried they might come into my room. So I didn't even lie down on the bed," Urrutia says.

At daylight, he went downstairs and noticed some individuals selling newspapers, and he bought one. He looked in the section SHIPS COMING AND GOING FROM BARCELONA, and what do you know? Exactly the ship he was looking for, the *Aldecoa,* was entering the port just about then. It was a Basque steamship from Bilbao, run by oil, newer, bigger, and a bit fancier than Urrutia's first ship. The important element was that he knew of two individuals from Galdakao working on it, because their brother had told him so. In fact, this guy had given Urrutia all the necessary information: where to go in Bilbao to apply for a job on a ship, what to do, etc. They called him *Mantxue* (One-armed person), though his last name was Zelaia. He had assured Urrutia, "If you ever get hold of that ship, my brothers will help you."

Hurrah for the Aldecoa*!*

By now, Urrutia had learned a few ropes regarding life on a ship, and he noticed the rope ladder dangling from the *Aldecoa.* He knew that the inspectors or the police were probably inside checking to see if the ship was carrying any contraband. Urrutia calmly climbed up the ladder and went inside. Nobody saw him. Acting like he knew what he was doing, he walked through the engine room, because on the other ships the kitchen was right close to the engine room. A fellow came in from the engine room and saw him.

"Who are you?" he asked.

"I am looking for Manuel Zelaia," Urrutia said.

"Well, that's me."

"Well, well, I know your brother in Galdakao."

"My brother? Where are you from? Galdakao? Who are your parents?"

When mutual acquaintances had been established, the man said, "What are you doing here? You got a business at home. You should be working with your folks."

Zelaia was from Uraburu, a hamlet up in the hills where Urrutia used to deliver feed with the donkey. Urrutia leveled with him and told him he was tired of the work in Galdakao and that he wanted a job on the ship. The *Aldecoa* man said that four individuals had jumped ship in the United States and they had been in need of help, but the captain had already called Bilbao where four new workers had been hired and presently they were on the train to Barcelona.

"I don't think you have any chance in here for a job," he said apologetically.

Urrutia wandered into the kitchen area. As he entered, he saw a man working and sweating. He look at Urrutia—I guess sometimes you can recognize a Basque face right away, even in Barcelona—and asked, "*Euskaldune?*"[2] (Are you Basque?)

"*Bai*" (Yes), answered Urrutia quickly.

"Just a second, I want to talk to you," he said.

The next thing Urrutia heard were the very same words he wanted to hear ever since he had left his ship in Huelva: "Are you looking for a job?"

"Yes, I am."

The cook told him that he was going to see the captain in order to fire the current helper he had, because he was dirty and lazy. He was referring to the other person standing in the kitchen, a Castilian, who didn't understand what they were saying. The cook wanted a Basque to work for him and to be his helper in the kitchen. Urrutia said that he would appreciate whatever he could do to get him a job. The cook went over and talked to the captain—who was also Basque—letting him know of his plan, but he opposed the idea. Then the cook said, "Well, I want to quit if you don't fire this guy. I got a good boy from my hometown here and I want to hire him."

The cook was from Gernika, Bizkaia. So finally the captain agreed, and the helper was let go and Urrutia moved in and took his place. Immediately, trying to put the fear of God in him, the cook said to Urrutia:

You'd better watch [out], because there will be lots of people coming to this ship looking for a job. You just keep busy, make them believe you have been working for a long time. If you don't, or if they think you are new, or somebody says you are, they will throw you overboard.

Urrutia did not agree with that: "Not me. At my age, they are not going to throw me overboard."

So he started cleaning the kitchen and peeling potatoes as diligently as he was able to. The cook was right: lots of individuals came around snooping in the kitchen area, but he just ignored them and applied himself to the task as if he were an old hand. He was determined to do the utmost not to jeopardize this godsent opportunity. Feeling a bit guilty, perhaps, the cook tried to reassure him:

"*Ez ardure, nik konponduko dot honek, ba'kit honen barri, da.*" (Don't worry, I will take care of these people, because I am aware of what is going on around here.)

First Sighting of the United States

After some time, the *Aldecoa* left Barcelona. It carried a cargo of lumber, which was unloaded in several Mediterranean ports, including Alicante, Spain. Then they proceeded to North Africa to take on a load, but Urrutia, who was applying himself to kitchen work, did not pay any attention to what they loaded. On his first trip across the Atlantic Ocean, the *Aldecoa* touched port in the southern United States, Tampa, Mobile, New Orleans, and Galveston. Before reaching Galveston, Urrutia had written to his stepbrother Manuel about going to Sabinas, Coahuila, Mexico, where he resided, because he thought that entering the United States from Mexico would be easier. In fact, in Galveston he made a deal with some Mexicans who were ready to escort him to Mexico. Besides taking a little money, they just asked him to put on some dirty clothes, and they assured him that crossing the border would not be a problem.

The ship was docked at Galveston for a month and a half, and during that time several letters crossed between Galveston and Coahuila. Manuel's letter said that Mexico was a tough and hot place. He worked in his uncle's business and managed the office for him. The letter advised Urrutia to avoid Mexico and try entering the United States through one of the eastern ports. Urrutia was disappointed because he had expected help from his stepbrother.

He guessed that Manuel did not feel comfortable with putting him to work as a simple worker while he was sitting in a big office. Or perhaps because there were no Basque people there, he thought Urrutia would not like it in Coahuila. Whatever the reason, let us keep in mind that the two had met just once, briefly at that, and that they were no blood relation. Urrutia thought to himself, "Well, if you don't want me, I won't go. If I wanted to be hard-headed I would just have gone to Coahuila and say 'hey, here I am.'" But Urrutia was not like that. (Yet, when Urrutia was living in Susanville, California, he drove down to Mexico once to visit Manuel.)

After finishing loading lumber, the *Aldecoa* headed again for Spain. By now, Urrutia was taking advantage of some of the knowledge he had acquired at sea. For example, risking falling off the ship, he used to hide an earthenware water container by hanging it under the lifeboats, where it kept at a cooler temperature. But working on the ship was a dirty business. The sleeping quarters were plagued with bedbugs, dark gray in color. They hid in the mattress, and they came out at night to eat you alive. Urrutia pulled his mattress out and slept on top of the deck, where it was cooler and the bugs didn't bother him too much.

They unloaded part of the cargo in the port of Seville[3] and other ports of southern Spain. They loaded the ship again and sailed to Ceuta and Tunis (Morocco and Algeria, respectively) in Africa, where they loaded cork. In Tunis they went to town, and when returning to the ship, they discovered that a number of men were sleeping on the docks and obstructing the pathway to the ship. The sailors had to jump over the slumbering men, and apparently in the process somebody stepped on someone, and soon angry Tunisians started chasing the mariners, who had to run for their lives. That was one part of Africa that Urrutia did not particularly enjoy.

The *Aldecoa,* with Urrutia on board, crossed the Atlantic with a load of cork for Wilmington, Delaware. It was about a year now that Urrutia had been sailing, which was his limit.

FOUR

Alien in a New Country: 1932

· · · · ·

To this day, the details of the early weeks and months in the United States are still etched in Urrutia's mind with great clarity. His adventure was just getting into high gear.

The captain of the *Aldecoa* called Urrutia to advise him of impending changes in his near future: "Young boy, did you know this is your last trip? I was looking at your naval card, and when we go with the ship to Spain, that's it."

The captain meant that Urrutia had to leave the *Aldecoa* and go into the Spanish navy for three years. It was inevitable, unless he did something about it. "This is it, it is tonight or never," he said to himself.

In Wilmington, the Immigration officers came onto the ship and took the names of the entire crew, which numbered about forty-five. Afterward, everyone was allowed to disembark. Promptly, most left ship to have a drink on dry land, go to a show, or whatever. Urrutia put on his suit, coat, and hat, but he left everything else on the ship. Taking anything along, such as his suitcase, would have been a dead give-away of his intentions.

Two Are Better Than One

This was the moment Urrutia had been waiting for. The best part was that he had nothing to lose. In the worst-case scenario, he would be caught and deported to Spain. He felt strangely powerful.

It was ten or eleven at night, and he separated from the

others who were going to have a beer. He was excited, to say the least, as he walked straight for the telephone office. He planned to call his friend Petralanda from Galdakao, who lived in New York City, but the excitement quickly turned into disappointment. He thought he would be able to hold a conversation in English with the operator, but he found out he could only manage to say a few words. Wondering about his next move, he left the telephone office and came face-to-face with a fellow crew-member, another Basque.

"What are you doing here?" he asked Urrutia.

"I want to call New York."

"What for?"

"I have a friend there."

"No, I think your intention is to leave the ship."

"Why?" Urrutia asked.

"Because I am, too. I am leaving the ship. So why don't you come with me. I am going to New York."

Emilio (Urrutia does not remember his last name) was from Bizkaia, born somewhere near Gernika, and since he had been in this country before, he could speak English pretty well. In fact, he told Urrutia that he made two trips across the Atlantic without paying a penny for them. Emilio asked Urrutia if he had any money, and he replied he had thirty-five or forty-five dollars, which he had exchanged his *pesetas* for with passengers going from the United States to Spain, thinking that some day dollars might come in handy. At the time the dollar and the *peseta* were about equal in value, Urrutia says. He gave Emilio the money and he bought train tickets to New York, where they arrived at Grand Central Station some two hours later at 2 A.M. Emilio advised him, "Walk straight and do not look to one side or the other, which would indicate that you are lost or new to the area. Follow me and pretend that you have been through this train depot for years."

Urrutia could handle that. He had been given similar advice by the cook on the *Aldecoa*. Emilio put him in a taxi, told the taxi driver where to go, paid him, and said good-bye. He was going across the bridge into Brooklyn, where he had a wife. Shortly, Urrutia arrived at the hotel owned by Valentin Aguirre.[1] He had given all the money to his friend, and he was now broke. At the hotel, everything seemed very quiet, and the night clerk asked him, "Are you deserting the ship?"

"Why are you asking?"

"If you are, I will just be nice to you, and I tell you not to register or sign your real name. Change your last name. FBI agents come and check these books every day, and they are going to catch you right now."

Urrutia thought about a friend he used to deliver coal to, whose last name was Idao (it matched Bilbao and Galdakao), and he registered as Ignacio Idao. The clerk gave him the key to the room and told him that he could talk with the hotel owner tomorrow to discuss his plans.

In the Big Apple

That was it. In New York City, one did not need any money to get a room. That was Urrutia's first pleasant surprise. The clerk said that was the policy of the hotel with the Basques who arrived with the intention to go west. As long as the guests had relatives in the United States, the owner would not deny lodging.

The next day, Urrutia came down to see the owner and saw quite a few FBI men in the lobby, because there had been a holdup just before he had arrived; some individuals with machine guns had robbed the place. He was told to return to his room and stay there, away from the FBI agents, until further notice. While waiting, he met another man from the Gernika area in Bizkaia. He was husky but young, and he was afraid. He, too, had jumped ship. Urrutia tried to cheer him up:

"What are you afraid of?" he asked him.

"I am going to Oregon," he said.

"Well, I am going to Idaho."

The fellow had a brother in Oregon and was waiting for him to send money so he could take the train across the country.

After some hours, they called Urrutia to come down to confer with the owner, Valentin Aguirre. He asked Urrutia where he was going, and he explained his situation: that he wanted to go to Boise, where his aunt lived, that she had a hotel, and that if he cared to call her up, she would pay for everything with a check or money order. The hotel owner agreed to do it, but as it turned out, by the time he took care of the matters of phone calls and train tickets, one whole week went by.

Urrutia was not particularly uncomfortable or unhappy in New York City. In fact, he had a good time. The hotel provided an interpreter for those who spoke no English, and every night he would go out on the town with the interpreter for two or three hours. They went to a club, had a beer or whiskey, and then returned to the hotel. The interpreter told him, "[As] long as you are with me nobody will touch you." Urrutia did not know what he meant by that. He was apprehensive about going out at night and wanted to stay inside, but the interpreter would say, "Don't worry. Nobody will bother you."

Compared to the Old Country, Urrutia found that the United States was more peaceful. That was his impression, because in Spain he had witnessed the exile of King Alfonso XIII as well as other disturbances. In spite of his alien status, which worried him for years, Urrutia says, "The United States treated me OK."

The interpreter/chaperon was with him only at night. During the day, however, he was nowhere to be seen. Maybe he was taking the other guests out and showing them around. It was a little strange, but whoever he was, Urrutia was happy that he was not the FBI. Urrutia stayed in his room all day long. He did not even look out the window, he was that apprehensive. He came out only for meals. The hotel had a beautiful dining room, where the meals were provided. "It was a first-class hotel," Urrutia recalls. Then, one day, the hotel owner called him and said, "I guess I have to put you on the road."

"Did you hear from my aunt?"

"Oh, yes. I got the money."

The Long, Dry Train Ride

Urrutia's aunt paid for everything, but Aguirre never gave him a bill so to this day he still does not know what his expenses were. In any case, Urrutia's adrenaline started flowing again. Mr. Aguirre, the hotel owner, told him he was going to be on the train for three days and three nights. He gave him a paper sack with two to three pounds of cheese and a lot of bread, and said, "It will hold you till you get to Boise, Idaho. And remember one thing, everybody leaves the train in Chicago. When you see everybody getting out, you follow them."

Thus, young Urrutia began the long train ride across the United States. The fellow Bizkaian going to Oregon was still stuck at the hotel, waiting. His brother might be sheepherding in the mountains, and who knows when the money would arrive! Urrutia had been luckier. His aunt lived in town with the telephone right next to her.

Urrutia took Aguirre's advice very seriously. He never left his seat until the train arrived in Chicago. He did not even go to the bathroom, and the trick, he said, was that he did not drink anything. He did not know where the bathroom was, anyway. He kept his gaze down or looked out the window. In case the immigration officers passed through the train, Urrutia had devised a plan of protection against detection. He had a suit and a hat on, so he was pretty well dressed. Furthermore, in order to better fit in and look like an American, he pretended to read a newspaper.

It must have been a long day and a half without drinking anything to wash the bread and the cheese down, but Urrutia was not complaining. Finally, the train stopped one more time, and everyone began to leave the train. Momentarily, Urrutia panicked, but he remembered Aguirre's words in New York City, "You are going to change trains in Chicago. And you better be sure, because there will be a lot of different directions you can take. So you be alert. Or if you got somebody to ask [tell him/her] that you want to go to Boise."

"So there were some people next to me riding from New York, and I tapped one fellow. I said something to him in Spanish, and he said, 'No I don't understand,' but he talked to his wife and his wife says, 'Yo hablo español' [I speak Spanish]. She had learned it in high school. 'Oh, you do?' Well, I'm safe," Urrutia thought, relaxing.

"I like go to Boise; which way should I go?"

"Well, you got to take this bus in here, and they will take you. You can come with us because we're going to California, and we will show you where the train for Idaho is."

Pretty soon, Urrutia saw the name Idaho. He said thank you to the people, and passing through the gate he got on the train. The conductor came in and checked his ticket. The conductor said to him, "Why don't you lie down?" It was night, and there was nobody in the seats that were facing each other. Urrutia took both seats and lay down to sleep.

He had worried so much about finding the right changeover in Chicago. Now this train would take him all the way to Boise. He could sleep at ease. The mere thought felt very comforting to him, though he was dying of thirst.

Daylight was breaking when the train pulled into Pocatello, Idaho. Urrutia knew that was Idaho, so he woke up with a rush, because as he figured it, Boise could not be very far now. The houses were almost totally covered by snow, and looking out the window to the frozen world of Pocatello made him feel like closing his eyes and returning back to sleep. He had hardly seen any snow in his life, and he said to himself, "My goodness, what kind of country did I come to? Is this how people live here?"

Urrutia had been on the train for more than two and a half days, and all along, in order to minimize detection, he had remained in his seat. The train was an unfamiliar environment to him. He worried that someone, or himself, might jump out or fall off the car. He did not go to the bathroom at all, which he accomplished by not drinking. Once in a while, he nibbled at the cheese he was given in New York City, and that was it. It was quite a sacrifice for him, because he was very thirsty and his legs felt cramped, but for someone in his predicament, quite worth it.

In Boise

When he arrived in Boise, we can only imagine what Urrutia was feeling. After what seemed like a lifetime of traveling, at last he had made it to his destination. Barely nineteen, he was ready to begin his life anew. So far, so good. At that moment, he wondered if all along "the Guy Upstairs was giving him directions. . . ."

The train left him quite a way off at one end of the Boise station. Stepping down onto the platform, he started walking toward the depot when he saw a uniformed man coming toward him, signaling with his hand. Urrutia panicked, thinking that he was a policeman, because he was dressed like one.

"Oh, no, they got me. The policeman. They got me," he said to himself.

So he turned around abruptly and started walking away from him. The uniformed man hollered, "*Euskaldune?*" (Are you Basque?).

Urrutia, startled but immensely relieved, answered, "*Bai*" (Yes) automatically and turned around to retrace his footsteps.

"Are you Urrutia?" the man asked.

"Yes."

After the initial exchanges, the man in uniform told Urrutia that he was a taxi driver. Urrutia quickly remarked that he had never seen taxi drivers dressed like that, with cap and all. "You scared [me] to death, I thought you were a policeman."

The Idahoan explained that in Boise every taxi driver wore that uniform and went on to say that for three days Urrutia's aunt had been sending him to the depot to meet the train and see if he found a stranger arriving from the East.

"I thought you were the one, the way you were walking and everything," the taxi driver said.

"I was tired sitting down for three days and three nights. I can hardly walk," Urrutia responded.

Indeed, it was a minor miracle that he still had enough saliva in him to be able to talk at all. He had hardly eaten and had not drunk a drop since New York.

The taxi driver took him to his aunt's *ostatu,* or boarding-house, Capital Rooms on Idaho Street. The place had thirty rooms, mostly rented to Americans, and the rest to Basques who were between jobs or spending a short vacation in town. They went upstairs, through the hall, and into the kitchen, and finally he met his aunt, Maria Urrutia. She was cooking with her partner, Cruza Arostegui—another Basque lady—at her side. He walked over his aunt and hugged her.

"You made it," she said.

"Thank God, I don't know how, but I am here."

"How did you do it?"

"It's a long story," he answered.

Maria Urrutia was married to Pedro Epelde, a foreman for John Achabal, a Basque sheepman. Epelde managed sheep camps and was not at home when Urrutia arrived. The Epeldes had three boys, Martin, Jose, and Luis. They were all tall, about the same age as Urrutia, and he found them sitting down in the kitchen. They looked like the photographs he had seen of them. They must have been expecting me, Urrutia thought with satisfaction.

The Epelde family, Ignacio Urrutia's adopted family in the United States. Left to right: Martin, father Pedro, Joe, Louie, mother Maria (Urrutia), and Ignacio, Boise, Idaho, 1935.

His aunt sort of lectured him on the situation he was faced with in Boise, and the available options:

> Now that you got this far, we don't want you to be sent back. The only thing for you to do is to go work in the mountains. Since you already changed your name, you won't have any problem. Use that name when you start working in the sheep.

Urrutia was not particularly excited with his aunt's plans, because in his own mind the object of his coming to the United States had included getting into some kind of business. Initially, he thought he wanted to be in the United States about ten years, after which he would return home with some money saved. Now his aunt wanted him to go hide in the mountains, even though he would have preferred to remain in town. Of course, on hindsight, Urrutia realizes that she was right, because the police had a lot of stool pigeons around.

He stayed in Boise a week, but it was not like the week in New York City, where he had a nice little vacation. His aunt did not allow him to go outside at all for fear of being detected. He saw nothing of Boise. He spent the days talking with his cousins and the few Basque guests. The owner-ladies ran the hotel. They cooked, too, but only for the Basque customers. Despite Prohibition, the boardinghouse served wine with the meals. Liquor cost $1 a shot, which was very expensive (sheepherders made $1 a day), but if caught, the owners paid stiff fines, Urrutia says, so they had to charge a lot for drinks.

Maria Urrutia bought him everything that a sheepherder might need on the range, like clothes and bedding, and before he knew it, she sent him away in search of a job in the little town of Emmett, less than fifty miles from Boise. He was accompanied by another Basque man, also looking for a job.

FIVE

Lonely Sheepherder: 1932–1936

· · · · ·

Urrutia did not know the first thing about sheepherding, and for the duration of the ride from Boise to Emmett he wondered if anyone in that business would give him a job. He wanted to stay in Boise and work in a store, but he guessed that his aunt knew better when she warned him of the dangers of remaining in Boise. Resigned, he psyched himself for the challenges ahead.

"Here We Spell It Idaho"

So the two prospective herders were driven to Emmett by pickup truck, and when they arrived they took lodging in the Basque boardinghouse. While waiting there, they saw a fellow come in, and Urrutia thought he had seen him in the Old Country. He walked up to him and said, "Excuse me, but I think I saw you riding the streetcar in Galdakao. I was driving my horse and wagon, and you were riding the streetcar."

"Well, that is right. I rode the streetcar several times, when I went back to see my sister in Galdakao. Who are you?"

They introduced themselves, and it turned out that the fellow knew Urrutia's family. The man was Maximo Zelaia, a native of Galdakao, now a foreman for a big sheep company.

"You want to work?" he asked.

"Yes."

"OK. I will come pick you up in the morning."

Zelaia, pointing at a building, told him to walk across the street to sign up at the office.

"How about my friend here?" Urrutia asked.

"I only need one herder," he answered.

Next morning, Urrutia walked over to the office as instructed, where he met a man about fifty years old with whiskers. His name was Andrew Little. When he gave his last name as Idao, Mr. Little told him that it was misspelled, "Here we write 'Idaho.'"

"Is that how you spell it?"

"Yes, that's how we write it in America."

So they added an *h* in the middle, and *Idao* became *Idaho*. It no longer rhymed with Galdakao and Bilbao—and of course *Idaho* is an Indian word that has nothing to do with the Basque *Idao*—but in the future, it would be part of Urrutia's life.

Thus, the very next day he started working for Andrew Little, Idaho's great sheepman. They instructed him to jump on the back of the truck, and he settled himself in the middle of the provisions being delivered to the sheepherders. It was minus thirty degrees outside, which combined with the speed of the truck made it more like minus seventy. Urrutia's clothes were quite inadequate for such temperatures, and he nearly froze to death. When they arrived at a ranch, he was stiff and had to be helped down from the truck and taken into the kitchen to warm up. He could hardly move his extremities.

"You are not used to this climate," they told him.

"Well, not [traveling] up on top of that truck," he answered.

They sat at the table to eat, and the dishes they brought over did not seem particularly enticing to him, except for one very red dish. Urrutia said to himself, "That, I am going to eat." So he took a heaping platter of it, but when he tasted it he found out they were beets, and he could not eat them. The foreman wondered why he had taken so much if he did not like them.

"I thought it was wine," Urrutia answered.

"That's no wine in there," the foreman said, laughing.

So Urrutia ate a piece of bread and returned to the back of the truck, even though, he says, there was room for him in the front cab. "That upset me. I was lucky to be alive."

Spring Lambing

As soon as they arrived in the camp, Urrutia received a crash course on sheepherding. It was February, lambing time in the foothills of Idaho. He was supposed to be working with the sheep, but he did not know anything about lambing. The weather was very cold, and when the lambs were born they were wet, and they could freeze in just a few minutes. So the herders worked day and night, twenty-four hours, trying to save the lambs from the cold weather. As soon as the ewes gave birth, the mothers with their lambs were taken inside a heated shed and put in individual pens. Occasionally, they missed a lamb that had been outside too long. When found, they tried to save it: they brought it inside near the stove, rubbed it to restart its circulation, and fed it a little warm milk. Sometimes they had to force open the half-frozen mouths to pour the milk inside; the warm liquid revived most of them.

That was something very new for Urrutia, but he said to himself, "This is what America is all about." During those days, he asked a lot of questions of his Basque coworkers about all aspects of the sheep operation. In fact, eventually he became an expert at lambing, which he did for eight years. The ewes sometimes had difficult births and had to be assisted. For example, when the lamb's black head appeared with the tongue out, the sheepherders had to move fast to save it. One herder with the sheephook tried to catch the ewe, and while another held the ewe down, a third herder went inside her with his hands and tried to grab the front legs of the lamb and, slow and easy, one leg at a time, pull it out. Even when at times you cannot grab both legs, pulling just one is enough to save the lamb. Other times, the lamb needs to be twisted inside before it can be pulled out, and during this operation the ewe might be bawling, really suffering. But once the lamb is born, you take it to the mother and presently she starts licking it and pretty soon both are alive and well.

At other times, the womb would come out and dangle from the back of the ewe. Once again, the herders had to hook her, put her down, and keep her from moving. A herder with a bucket of clean warm water tried to clean the womb as best as possible and then gently return it inside. To prevent the uterus from spilling back out, the opening was tied with a string and the mother was often saved. But not always.

After lambing was over—in Idaho, that was from about April 1 to April 10—the sheep were taken into the sage-brush country where tender green grasses were sprouting. Then they were moved higher to the corrals, where shearing took place, and the male lambs were docked or castrated. The shearers were professionals, and they might take a week or more to complete the job. In the meantime, the herders tried to stay busy doing various chores.

During his first weeks with the sheep, in spite of finding himself in unfamiliar surroundings, Urrutia took things in stride. As he said,

> I never looked back. I was looking ahead at what was coming to me, at what I had to do. I was in a different country, and I knew things would be different. For two years I did not come to town. Andrew Little was a Scotsman. They called him Mandy, and he owned 100,000 head of sheep. He was a multimillionaire then.

I met him in the office when I went to give my name. He treated me like he was my father. He said that he wanted me to work for him, because he had a lot of Bascos working for him. He must have had over a hundred Bascos working in his outfit.

Counting Sheep

When shearing was over in April, Urrutia was put in charge of three thousand head of ewes and lambs and sent to the low hills. It was not a single band but the tail ends of all the sheep of the company, some big, some small, some bums, all kinds, which were going to different mountain ranges. He was told that he might have problems (such sheep are harder to herd than a single band is), but he did not know what they meant by *problem*.

Now, finally, he was another Basque sheepherder in the United States. They gave him a hat, three dogs, a .30-.30 rifle, camp gear, and cooking utensils, and they left him in the mountains by himself. The first thing he had to do was to devise a camp strategy. He looked around and he thought, "No more maids to do the laundry and the cooking." Fortunately, he knew how to cook a little, because he had learned at sea.

The sheep were all over the mountains, but he let them be. Whenever the coyote was killing in the night, he packed his bed and carried it to the ridges, where he slept, changing places each night. But Mr. Coyote was smart, and he would kill at the bottom of the canyon sometimes eight, nine, or ten lambs. Urrutia worried about that. He also saw bears and cougars in the high country.

One day, a month or two later, a foreman named John Guerry[1] showed up and said to Urrutia, "*Gazte, ardiek kontau ein biuz. Ardi baltzak kontau ozuz?*" (Young fella, we need to count the sheep. Have you counted the black sheep?)

Ignacio Urrutia and his sheep camp while employed by Andrew Little of Emmett, Idaho, 1934.

"*Ez*" (No), Urrutia answered.

"*Kanpaiak p'ez?*" (Not even the bells?)

"*Ez.*"

"Where are your sheep?" Guerry inquired.

"All over the mountains," replied Urrutia.

"Well, you'd better go [find them]. I'll go up this way, and you go up that way and let us bring them down here."

When the roundup was complete, they started counting and he was short about 1,200 head. Urrutia was stunned. They were gone, all right, but he had no idea where. The foreman advised him to gather the sheep in one bunch in one area every night, and the next day to get going before the sheep started moving out on their own.

"Nobody ever told me that," Urrutia said.

He was learning the hard way. The foreman went out looking for the stray sheep, and finally about a week later he showed up with them. Guerry told him, "Young fella, you'd better keep an eye on the sheep. What you ought to do is count the black and count the bells. And that way you know if you lose them. Count them every day. If you miss one black, that means a bunch of sheep are missing."

Urrutia did not know, since no one had taught him how to count sheep. He was grateful to the foreman and promised to do as he was told.

Guerry proceeded to see the next sheepherder, a fellow from Bermeo, Bizkaia, and he told him all about Urrutia's problems, adding that his career as a sheepherder would probably be short.

His summer range was above McCall, Idaho, on one of the highest mountains in the area. It was beautiful country with lots of grass. He trailed the sheep for five days, over and across the West Mountains where they had ten to twelve feet of snow. Going over was not so easy for the sheep. They had to cross big creeks, and some of the lambs were swept away by the rushing waters. But when Urrutia reached the

Sheepherding in the summer range, McCall area, Idaho, 1934. Observe that, unlike urban hikers today, Ignacio Urrutia is protected against the elements.

valley on the other side of the mountains, he found nice green grass, and the sheep rested for one day. The grass was so tall you could hardly see the sheep in it. The next day he resumed the trail toward his summer range, which became his home for three months, from June through August.

Sheepherders carved trees during the summer months in the mountains. In this photograph, a herder named Urrutia left his mark on a tree, 1960.

The herder next to his range, Florencio—everyone called him Bermeo—came over one day to Urrutia's camp for dinner and repeated the news he had heard from Guerry. "I don't think you are going to be staying in this company very long, because you lost so many sheep."

Urrutia did not like what he was hearing, but that was OK. He wanted to go to Boise anyway and get a different job.

"They found the sheep," Urrutia defended himself.

"Yeah, but you see, you neglected them; you don't even know how many days they were up there by themselves."

"Well, I did not know how to herd them. It is my first year."

Surprise!

In spite of the shaky start, that summer Urrutia redeemed himself by outdoing even seasoned herders. In August when the sheep converged in the corrals from which the lambs were to be shipped, Mr. Little was at hand surveying the operation. He looked the lambs over and poked them with his cane as a way to check their plumpness. As it turned out, Urrutia's lambs were the biggest ones in the company. Mr. Little inquired about the identity of the herder, and he was told that it was the guy who had lost a bunch of sheep.

"But finally he learned how to watch them," foreman Guerry said.

Urrutia was pleasantly surprised. He had no idea his lambs could be the heaviest, because he did not have any experience. His method was to let his charges wander about. Experts believe that such an approach is a lot less stressful on the sheep, and it certainly worked in Urrutia's case. He was tickled pink for proving Bermeo wrong. "I think I did pretty good, because they told me that I raised the biggest lambs," he told him.

It turned out that Bermeo was let go after the lamb shipping, but Urrutia was given a herd of dry ewes to take back to the mountains. He still had a job after all. He did not care one way or another. He would have liked to go to town like Bermeo, because the sheepherder's job is a lonely one. Nevertheless, he also began to enjoy the mountains more than before: the clean, clear water, the abundance of grass, and the lack of worry. When there is a lot of pasture, the sheep do not move much, and the herder has lots of free time. The job is not difficult, and being alone did not bother him too much.

Urrutia's other neighbor herder was an American from Tennessee, who at times, like Bermeo, visited his camp. In fact, Little's outfit employed several herders from Tennessee. Whenever they got together, Urrutia tried to be a good host and started cooking something like beans, eggs, or ham. In the meantime, the Tennessean pointed at objects and said *plate, fork, knife,* etc., and Urrutia tried to repeat the words. That is how he began to learn English, little by little, because with the Basques he only spoke Euskara.

Unlike most other sheepherders in the American West, Urrutia had no burro and no horse (though, occasionally the camptender brought a horse for him to ride). About once or twice a month, the camptender came in with the provisions and moved camp at the same time. He had three pack mules and the horse he rode. The herder did not have to bother about moving camp, but he did have to gather his own firewood for the stove, which was usually located inside the tent. The smoke was exhausted through a small pipe. However, during the hot summer months, the stove might be moved outside the tent.

One camptender Urrutia remembers was Tony Bullshit.[2] That was his nickname, because he loved to talk a lot and, besides, he had a hard time telling the truth. He was Bizkaian, and his last name was Arrubarrena. Another individual he remembers from his sheepherding days was Tony Basabe, who was a sharp, well-dressed fellow and, along with his cousin Johnny Basabe, one of the top managers in Andrew Little's sheep operations.[3] Basabe eventually married Urrutia's girlfriend, Dominga, but we are getting ahead of our story.

Food and Daily Routine

Urrutia learned to be a sheepherder, which included doing all kinds of chores. For baking the famous sheepherder bread, he opened a trench with the shovel, where he built a fire. By then, the dough was rising for the second time in the Dutch oven. When the fire subsided into a nice bed of coals, the lamb stew with potatoes and peppers was first cooked. Then the bread went in the trench, and the Dutch oven was covered with a layer of dirt to maintain the heat. After an hour or so, the big, round, golden loaves were ready to be eaten. Great big slabs were cut and dipped into the rich sauce of the stew. "Natural food, the best you have ever eaten," says Urrutia, reminiscing about his years on the range.

His diet lacked variety, however, and fresh fruits and vegetables. Beside bread, the staples were rolled oats, eggs, macaroni, and canned goods. The oats and the flour came in fifty-pound sacks. The eggs were kept in a box. One time, he had over thirty dozen eggs in the camp. He cooked several dozen and gave most of the omelet to the dogs. There was no dog food back in Urrutia's time. Dogs ate what the herder ate. With canned tomatoes he made jelly by adding water and sugar and cooking the mixture in low heat. He had canned milk, sugar, and rice, but he did not cook rice pudding, which growing up in Bekelarri he used to gobble up.

Urrutia often repeats that one reason he had left home was the hard work he had endured at an early age, lifting and delivering one-hundred-pound sacks. He discovered that the United States was more than he had expected: "When I came here, I found out that life was much easier. I cooked my own bread and lamb in the Dutch oven, eat good, and [there was] nobody to boss me around. I made $30 a month, of which I sent $20 home."

Urrutia's routine during the lonely summer months began before daybreak, at 5 A.M. or earlier. Many herders made coffee before tending the sheep, but Urrutia did not. The herder must rise before the sheep start stirring, so that he can direct them to a particular pasture; otherwise, they might scatter all over. He returned to camp about 10 A.M. for his first meal of the day, a combination of breakfast and lunch. He always kept some food ready, so all he had to do was warm it up.

After eating, he stayed busy with different chores, such as chopping firewood, doing laundry, shaving, baking, or taking a siesta. There was little need to clean house or to make the bed, "but you had to watch for rattlesnakes inside the bed."

During the heat of the summer, the sheep do not eat but lay down in the shade. When it cools in the afternoon, they start feeding again, at which time the herder returns to his job. In the evening, he makes sure the sheep bed down in a good place, to lessen the chances of attack by predators or heading in the wrong direction in the morning.

The camptender came about every one or two weeks, bringing the mail and the provisions. It was an important visit, because he not only brought news from the outside world but moved the sheepherder's camp as well.

Urrutia had two Australian shepherd dogs, Shorty and Pinto, who in spite of their names understood one language only, Basque. Urrutia would command them: "*Ekarri harek*" (Bring them in), and they went around the herd and drove the sheep in. In fact, Urrutia brushed up his own Basque in the sheep camps. In Galdakao, he had neglected it, and when he went to herd sheep, in the beginning they called him *maketo* (a derogatory term for Spanish or non-Basque), and he did not like that. He applied himself in earnest, and Euskara came back to him quickly. He also tried to read American newspapers.

Two Stories and a Check

In an interview conducted in May 1999, I asked Urrutia if he had—like most other Basque herders—carved aspen trees in the high country. "I don't remember, but I am sure I did. I saw a lot of names which others carved on trees in Idaho," he said. Carving their name, dates, and human figures, especially women, was one of the sheepherder's pasttimes during the summer months. There are thousands of trees carved in this manner.

Left to right: Juan Bilbao, Ignacio Urrutia, and Morga. See Urrutia's 1928 Chevrolet Coupe (left). McCall area, Idaho, 1937. (See discussion on page 81.)

Urrutia told of the time when he was all alone in the summer range and one day the strangest thing happened: a car with three ladies in long dresses drove up the mountain, and when they saw him, they stopped the car and got out. They started asking him questions, but he did not understand English and all he could say was "No, no, no," shaking his head at the same time. Sheepherders used to desperately long for women, but when a real one came close, they often froze. The cultural and linguistic barriers were too great for them.

Another time, he had a close encounter with a large mammal. There were many bears in the mountains around McCall, and they could be dangerous. The sheepherders set traps for them, which Urrutia calls "shoots," consisting of a bait that was tied to a gun's trigger. When the bear started eating the meat, the gun went off, killing it. Urrutia had a rifle and a six-shooter with him, but on the day he came face-to-face with a bear, he had no gun with him. The black bear was huge and kept staring at him, but strangely refused to move. Urrutia looked for a rock to throw, but there was not any. He knew he could not outrun the bear, and as he was deciding what to do, he was intrigued that the bear was not moving at all. That gave him courage, and he took off to get his gun. When he returned with the rifle, the bear was gone. "Bears can smell gunpowder," he says. He found two dead sheep nearby, and then he understood why the bear was not moving: he had a full stomach, which made him lethargic.

After he worked two years for Little's sheep company, he came to town intending to make a quick trip to Boise to see his aunt and the uncle whom he had not yet met. Urrutia told his boss about his wish to take two weeks off to visit his relatives in Boise, and subsequently he was handed a paycheck for $250. The sheepherders were making $30 a month, and even though he had been sending money home and the company made deductions for clothes and other necessities, Urrutia thought that he had more money coming to him—he knew his numbers. He was in the main office of the company in Emmett, Idaho, facing Andrew Little himself, and he told him that the dollar amount in the check was not correct. Mr. Little said, "Young fellow, if you are not satisfied with the check I gave you, I am going to call the Immigration officers and turn you in."

Urrutia understood what Little meant very clearly, because the Immigration people were on his mind all the time. So he grabbed the check and left quickly, and he never went to work for that company again.

Sheepmen Go Broke

From Emmett he went to Boise and gave the check to his aunt, apologizing that the amount probably was not enough, and his aunt agreed but she added, "This won't pay for what I send, but you shouldn't worry about it.

You go back to work—there is lots of work here—you can go to work for any company, and when you make some more money, you pay me." Urrutia recalls that she never told him how much she sent to New York and what the expenses were. But in any case, after that she never asked for any more money, and that was the end of it.

Whenever he went to town and stayed in her boarding-house, he paid for the room, food, and everything else. There was nothing free. In those days, people made a dollar a day, so there was not much money to spare. That is why Urrutia did not visit town too often, or when he did he did not stay too long. Cost was one reason, the other being the police, the FBI, etc. If a person like him were to get into trouble for whatever reason, he could be shipped out of the country in a flash.

As provincial as Boise might have been in the early 1930s, for the sheepherders it was, nevertheless, a big and exciting town. One interesting feature was the whorehouses, located right on the main street. In spite of such amenities, Urrutia was a driven man, and in short order he announced to his aunt that he was "going up to the hills." He took another job with a different sheep company.

After he quit his job in Emmett in 1934, he worked two more years as a full-time sheepherder. One outfit was that of Wesley Crookshank in Montour, which is just a hill with one house on it near Emmett. He worked for him for one year or so. Then in 1936 he worked for Manu Mochis, a Basque. He had one band of sheep. He enjoyed working for him, because Mochis was with him in camp all the time. He did not practice transhumancy but rented meadows for the sheep, nice clean ones. One morning they saw black cars coming, and Mochis said to him, "I think we have a problem. I think the bank is coming to take my sheep."

"The bank?"

"Yeah. You see, here the bank takes the sheep away if you don't pay back the loan."

Incidentally, Urrutia adds, a lot of the sheep companies went broke—those were Depression years, after all. Indeed, the bank people took Mochis's sheep, and Urrutia was out of a job.

Mochis advised him to go to town. In fact, he offered to take him there, which he accepted. The town was Cascade, close to McCall, and he took a room in the Basque boardinghouse in town. He could do little but stay there until another job came along. Mochis felt bad for Urrutia, because he knew it was the wrong time to look for another job tending sheep. Besides, scores of sheepmen were going broke. What was Urrutia, an alien in a strange country, going to do?

War in the Basque Country: 1936–1939

The 1930s decade in the United States was a tough one economically but could hardly be compared with the misfortune that befell the Basque Country. In Hegoalde (Spanish Basque Country) the Civil War raged for three years (1936–1939), while in Iparralde (French Basque Country) Hitler's Nazis occupied France (1940–1945). Before we proceed to the next chapter in Urrutia's life, we must pause to talk about these fundamental events that affected the Basques. The Civil War claimed one million dead in Spain, among them Urrutia's classmates and friends in Galdakao. Another million were forced to leave the country. The holy city of the Basques, Gernika, was bombed and burned by the Nazi airplanes fighting with Franco's forces. The destruction was immortalized by Picasso in *Guernica,* one of his masterpieces.

The mail was slow but kept Urrutia abreast of the course of the war, which affected his stepfamily in Galdakao deeply.

His stepbrother Josemari was a general with the Republican army protecting Galdakao when the so-called African or Moroccan troops under General Franco terrified the Basque Country. The army of the democratically elected government had very little to fight with against a superior force equipped by Mussolini and Hitler.

At the time, the Diego family was building a new three-story structure half a mile west of the town plaza, that is, toward Bilbao, with funds provided by Manuel Diego in Mexico. But the Italians bombed it; they also bombed the family bedrooms up on the hill, which had to be rebuilt. Eventually, the family business was moved to a new place, where on the ground floor Fernando Diego set up his own feed store.

In Idaho, Urrutia was getting letters from home and learned that Josemari had been captured by Franco's forces and taken to Santander. He was imprisoned there and was scheduled to be executed. Fortunately, a letter of recommendation from the priest in town saved him after it was forwarded to Franco. But something happened to him, probably the stress of being in prison for six months, and his black hair turned white as snow. After the war, he worked in a bank in Bilbao, and he died a short time later.

During the war, the Diego family went into hiding in Cantabria, in the native hamlet of Francisco Cano, their hired hand, who was raised in the mountains. Later, during one of his trips back to Spain, Urrutia visited the house and the hamlet where the family hid during the war. No army went there, and the family was safe all the time. The end of the war signaled a new policy of incredible repression against the Basques and their culture. In a latter chapter, Urrutia talks about the aftermath of Franco's dictatorship.

SIX

In Logging Camps: 1936–1940
· · · · ·

The owner of the boardinghouse in Cascade, where Urrutia was staying, suggested he check out a nearby logging camp to inquire about a job. The man had a car and could have driven Urrutia to the camp, but he knew Urrutia did not have any money to pay him, so instead he advised the young Basque to walk across the valley and over the hills to the place where smoke coming out of the timber could be observed.

"Some Bascos are working up there. They work for this Austrian guy," he told Urrutia.

"I don't care where he is or how far, I just want to get a job," Urrutia said gratefully and started walking.

Urrutia walked across the valley and crossed irrigation ditches and canals with some difficulty. As he walked, he realized that all along he had missed people's company. The idea of a logging camp was more attractive to him than a sheep camp. Looking from far away at those pine-forested mountains, he wondered what it would be like to be a logger, to cut down those big trees. He figured now he might have a chance to find out.

Didn't You Hear Me Holler?

He finished walking through the valley and proceeded into the timber. When he thought he was close to the work area, he heard a noise, but he did not see anybody. Something, instinct perhaps, told him to go behind a big tree, and suddenly all hell broke loose around him. The ground was spitting dirt, rocks, and debris. After the dust subsided, he came around the tree and caught sight of a fellow who was staring at him with a puzzled look.

"Where were you?" he asked.

"Behind that tree."

"Boy, didn't you hear me holler? I said 'fire!' "

"I didn't understand what you were saying. I heard the noise, but I didn't know what it was. I knew there was something dangerous, because I didn't see anybody around."

"You could have been killed in a place like this," the man said.

They were dynamiting the grade to build a railroad. Urrutia excused himself as best as he could and asked the dynamite man for directions to the site where the crew was working. He was directed to walk farther back and told that when he heard noises of shovels and hammers he would know he was getting close. So he started walking back when he saw this big man throwing dirt in the grade with his big boots as he walked. He was the contractor, a four-hundred-pound Austrian, and he walked like a duck with his feet pointed to the sides. When he saw Urrutia, he asked him, "What are you doing here?"

"I am looking for some friends."

"Are you Basque?"[1]

"Yes."

"What do you want?"

"I want a job."

"Job? I have a lot of Basques working for me. Go talk to them."

Urrutia left him and went back to the place where the Basque crew was shoveling the dirt into the railroad tracks. There were about fourteen, among them Juan Bilbao, Frank Bilbao, Louie from the town of Eibar,

Jauregui nicknamed "Morga," and others. After the initial greetings and the obligatory question "*Nungo'az?*"[2] (Where are you from?), he related to them his conversation with the Austrian.

"Did you ask him for a job?"

"Yes, I did, but he told me to come talk to you guys."

"You will get a job. He will give you one," they reassured him.

Building Railroads

After a while, the boss arrived and asked the Basques what they thought of Urrutia.

"You'd better hire him," one of them said.

Without further ado, the Austrian told Urrutia to show up for work the next morning. Urrutia was thrilled to hear it, because he not only needed the job, he enjoyed working in the company of people. In high spirits, he walked back across the valley and into Cascade. He went to the boardinghouse to pick up his stuff and proceeded to move to the logging camp.

This was a typical logging camp owned by the Boise-Payette Lumber Company. It contained living quarters and eating facilities for the workers, totaling about two hundred. The next morning, Urrutia put his bedding in one of the bunkhouses and continued to the cookhouse to eat, after which he went to work.

His crew numbered seventeen and was building a railroad bed. Whenever the tracks had to cross a creek or a river, they built a bridge first. This was going to be quite a learning experience for the store clerk and delivery man turned seaman, turned sheepherder. He did not understand enough English yet, and when someone asked him, "Get me the shovel," he tried to guess the question and brought the pick. When asked to bring the hammer, he

Scenes from Ignacio Urrutia's years with the Boise-Payette Lumber Company, ca. 1936–1940.

would bring the bar, and so on. The boss was kind of impatient with him and he hustled him, suspecting that Urrutia was simply playing games, until one of the Basques reminded the Austrian that he was a bit too rough with the newcomer:

"You should not treat that boy like that. He is young and he doesn't know what he is doing."

Indeed, Urrutia was the junior in the bunch.

"The only reason I am pushing him around is because one of these days he is going to beat you guys in this business," said the Austrian.

The Basque fellow later confided to Urrutia, "I talked with the boss about you, and he said that he is being tough on you because he thinks you will be a good man for him."

In fact, it was not six months before he became leader of the bunch by being appointed record-keeper for the seventeen men in his crew. At the end of each period, he handed the time sheets to the Austrian, who wrote the checks accordingly. Not everyone was happy with his rapid ascent, especially the more lazy ones, because Urrutia

Left to right: Juan Bilbao, Ignacio Urrutia, unidentified, and "Morga" (from the town of Morga, Bizkaia), standing on the railroad tracks they built for the Boise-Payette Lumber Company. Their employer supplied them with half-gallon bottles of Olympia Beer, which they enjoyed after a long, hard summer workday, Cascade area, Idaho, 1937.

pushed them on the job mercilessly and they did not like that. He became the fastest man driving the railroad spikes. He and Juan Bilbao made a team driving the spikes. Urrutia recalls, "We sweated like crazy, water pouring out our shirts. You had to work like a slave, because there were guys waiting to see if you quit to take your job."

Urrutia worked for his Austrian boss every summer

until 1940. In the spring, he didn't have to ask for a job, he simply showed up at the camp.

Sometimes the railroad builders were involved in unexpected jobs, like once in 1936 when there was a forest fire in northern Idaho and all were trucked to the site to help the firefighters. After long hours on the road, they finally arrived at their destination, and they built trenches and fire lines until the fire was contained. The whole time Urrutia suffered from a bad headache, which he attributed to the smoke.

Part-Time Herder

When the snow season came in November, logging became impossible and they were laid off. That is when he went back to the sheep camps. During lambing time (December–April), sheepmen needed all the help they could get, and there were several outfits that he worked for. One was John Achabal, the largest Basque sheep owner in Idaho, who had many partners. Urrutia worked for one of them, Johnny Mendiola, one April during lambing. He hauled hay for the lambs in the shed. One time when he was climbing on the wagon, one of the mules kicked him and injured his ankle. He had to go to the doctor and stay in town until his ankle was healed.

Another season he was hired by Chacartegui, a Basque company that had a ranch in Nampa, Idaho. He obtained the job thanks to their distant kinship with his aunt. The Chacarteguis employed him during winter time and during spring lambing, while the sheep were kept in sagebrush territory. Beyond April, they did not need him because the Chacarteguis had several boys of their own who herded sheep within fenced meadows, which incidentally were located very close to Urrutia's logging camp. The arrangement was just right for him. Besides, working for the Chacarteguis was like a family affair.

Sometime around 1936 he bought a car, a 1928 Chevrolet Coupe. During the months he worked for the Chacarteguis, he parked it in a little shed where the car just fit and was covered and protected. One day, he gave a ride to a Basque named Angel, who had obtained a job in a power plant on the Snake River. He drove over sagebrush until they reached the canyon ledge and saw the river down in the distance.

The road leading to the power plant was steep and looked like a snake. Urrutia figured that he did not need any power to go downhill and thought that by turning the engine off and selecting high gear, the vehicle would actually reduce the speed. He began coasting down and soon found out otherwise. The car raced toward the river, and it quickly became quite obvious that he had better negotiate those tight curves or else. Meanwhile, his passenger was struggling to hang onto his seat. For a few short minutes, it was quite a ride, but finally they made it to the bottom of the hill. The scared yet grateful passenger said thank you, and a few minutes later departed. Urrutia drove out of the river canyon, and when he reached the top of the hill his car was overheating. There was no water in the radiator, so he walked a couple of hours to a ranch to get a bucket of water (there were no plastic milk jugs back then).

As indicated, for four years Urrutia had two main seasonal jobs, logging and lambing, which afforded him relaxing intervals of short vacations in town. He was a gregarious young man and, though he generally disliked the smoky pool hall crowd, he made friends, some of them women. Often, Old Country neighbors, or those born in the same area, were likely to become friends in the New World. Maria Urrutia (Mrs. Epelde) had such a lady friend, who owned a ranch with dairy cows in the Boise valley. Through his aunt, Ignacio Urrutia secured a temporary job milking cows at the ranch. As compensation, he was getting free room and board. This was the 1937–1938 winter, when he was collecting $27 a week for unemployment.

Urrutia befriended Dominga, the daughter of the ranch lady. In fact, his aunt Maria urged him to marry her, because Dominga's mother and she were from the same area in Gipuzkoa. She later married Tony Basabe, as mentioned earlier.

Logging-Camp Work

During the four years he was employed in logging camps, one of the primary tasks was building railroads and laying down the tracks. Building a railroad bed in steep mountain terrain was quite a chore. The train that ran on the tracks was owned by the same outfit, Boise-Payette Lumber Company, and it could pull maybe twenty to thirty cars loaded with logs. But whenever the ground became soggy from rain or moisture, the tracks often moved under the weight, or worse, the train sometimes tipped over. Whenever that happened, day or night, the building crew was rushed to the scene to fix the tracks. With the help of the big cranes that were brought to the site, the train was lifted back onto the tracks.

The main office of the Boise-Payette Lumber Company was located in Boise, but Urrutia's logging camps were mostly around Cascade. The first camp he worked at was Cabarton, and from there he moved to New Meadows, which is past McCall in northern Idaho. The crews were transported in a big truck, and the ride from the living quarters to the work place might take a while, two or three hours sometimes. They worked long hours, averaging ten or twelve hours, six days a week.

Sometimes they worked Sundays for extra money, but normally Sundays were reserved for washing clothes and other menial chores. Laundry was done by hand in a special area in camp, equipped with sinks, hot and cold water, scrubboards, brushes, etc. The clothes were hung to dry. Each man took care of his own clothes. They cleaned their bunkhouses as well, which were railroad cars with cots in them. Twelve people were assigned to each car. The cookhouse was located in another car, but some camps had their own cookshack outside.

Tons of Food

In the mornings when the logging site was a considerable distance away, the bell rang at 5 A.M. The men had to get up promptly and head out for the breakfast table. During the hot days of summer time, the first thing they did after waking up was to drink beer, which came in half-gallon containers. The Austrian tried to keep his crew happy and provided beer for them, and he did not skimp on food, either. For breakfast, they might eat cereal, hot cakes, eggs, fruit, milk, and coffee—as much as they wanted. The milk came straight from the surrounding farms.

They took lunches along in a pail. While working on the railroad tracks, their lunch was a ham sandwich. Urrutia still remembers it vividly because he enjoyed it a lot. The cook was an older fellow and he built the fire by the tracks. He put a large frying pan over it with three to four pounds of butter to melt, and then he added ham slices into the melting butter. When they were nice and hot, he slapped the meat between two large pieces of fresh bread that had been baked at the cookhouse. He made a premium hot sandwich that was enjoyed with coffee by all the seventeen members of the crew. For dessert, they opened gallon cans of fruit, such as plums, pears, etc. Urrutia recalls that many people did not eat the fruit, but he loved it. "I am crazy about fruit," he says. Between meals, the crew took coffee into the field in a thermos

Ignacio Urrutia sweeps the railroad car, which served as a bunkhouse for the workers of the Boise-Payette Lumber Company. It is here that he taught the citizenship classes to his coworkers, 1937.

bottle, which was much appreciated when the temperature outside was minus twenty degrees.

The food was great, but work was hard and the days long. The foreman never looked at his watch. They went according to the daylight. Typically, they started working at 7 A.M. and quit at 6 P.M. The foreman drove them hard in order to finish the job on time. "He was worried all the time, scratching his head, that he was not going to make it," Urrutia says. But there were rewards at the end of the day. In the creek, hidden under the willows, the Austrian kept cold beer, which not surprisingly was much appreciated after a long hot day. It was Olympia Beer in half-gallon glass containers. "We drank that half gallon in a hurry," Urrutia says.

By the time the crew returned to camp for supper, it was between 7 P.M. and 8 P.M. People were tired and hungry. For supper, they had everything, from soup to steaks, including salad and fresh pies, washed down with coffee and milk. The camp had two cooks and several women who waited on the tables. Urrutia describes the scene at suppertime:

> We kept those girls busy just bringing the milk. They worked so hard . . . they brought pitchers of milk. We had an appetite, boy, we ate like horses. They brought heaping plates, and they were empty in a flash. They

Ignacio Urrutia the logger, undercutting for the Boise-Payette Lumber Company, near Cascade, Idaho, 1936.

refilled them, and again we emptied them. They kept bringing some more. That was one thing: we were never short on food. The wages were not great— thirty-five cents an hour, and no tax—but we ate as much as we wanted. The cost of the food was reasonable, $1 day, which was deducted from our paycheck.

After supper the crew retired to the bunkhouses to smoke and chat a bit before dozing off. Urrutia recalls that it was smoky in there. He never smoked and he hated it. Still, sleeping was never a problem. Although the bunkhouses were not particularly toasty warm, little stoves kept them from becoming uncomfortably cold, and besides, each person could throw on his bed as many blankets as he wanted. Nobody needed sleeping pills, that is for sure.

School for the Illiterate in the Forest

There were Yugoslavians, Germans, Czechoslovakians, Austrians, and Hungarians in his bunkhouse, Urrutia being the only Basque. The work crews and the bunkhouse crews were not the same. During the period between supper and bedtime, there were intervals of animated conversation on a variety of topics. One evening, a fellow held a book in his hand and proposed the following question:

"Hey, Idaho [everybody called Urrutia by that name], why don't you give us a few lessons from this book?"

The title was—as best as Urrutia can remember—*United States Citizenship,* and it contained questions and answers about the Constitution and government of the United States. The man had obtained it in Boise and brought it to the camp. They all wished to become citizens someday, and they knew they had to become familiarized with the contents of the book in order to pass the citizenship test.

Urrutia leafed through the book and after some thought

agreed to be the instructor. He was the most educated among the bunch—some were actually illiterate and none could read English. Taking the book in his hands, he settled himself in his bunk. He always slept on the top bunk bed. The book was about a hundred pages long and contained questions and answers designed for the immigrants who applied for citizenship. At this time, Urrutia had not formulated any plans to become a citizen yet, but he thought that perhaps some day the answers in the book might be useful to him. He was right, but he didn't know it just then.

As serious as a real teacher in a real school, he developed a routine: from the book he read a question aloud and waited for an answer. When none was forthcoming, he read the answer. After several tries, most of the workers memorized the correct answers, after which Urrutia quizzed individuals around the bunkhouse.

There was this fellow, about seventy years old, sitting in the lower bunk. He did not do much work, some cleanup here and there . . . he was a good friend of the boss. His name was Joe Cook, and one evening, during a teaching session, he said to Urrutia, "Idaho, why don't you ask me an easy question?"

"OK. Who is the president of the United States?"

Joe had a little moustache and he kept stroking it, thinking, thinking of an answer. Everybody was quiet, and finally Joe said, "You know, Idaho, that's a hard question."

Urrutia was stern: "Maybe it is for some people, but you should know it. You live in this country . . . you should know these things."

Urrutia was getting a kick out of seeing the expression on Joe Cook's face. Suddenly, he seemed to feel guilty. "By God, I cannot even think of the name of the president."

Old Joe never became a citizen, but all the others in Urrutia's "classroom" did. In the process of being the instructor, Urrutia learned the entire book by heart. He learned about the Congress and the Senate, the Representatives, and all that. His training in "bunkhouse teaching" came in very handy later on. However, to this day, Urrutia cannot forget the one question he was asked during his citizenship exam that was not in the book. He could not answer it, but we will get to that later.

Some of the names of the fellows who shared the bunkhouse and took classes from him were Mike Simonich, Mike Gulsey, Joe Cook, Sam Ecovich, the cook, and. . . That is all he could remember momentarily, but he added, "Most of them live in Boise, and I can get those names, probably every one of them, because I was familiar with them."

Falling Timber

Typically, the job in the logging camp lasted from May until the first heavy snow. For the most part, they built roads for the log train, but when the weather turned nasty, they quit grading and concentrated on laying the track for as long as they could, that is, until the ground became too wet or frozen. At that time, they gave up their shovels and picked up their axes and band saws to become loggers. Their job description changed, but they were still working for the same company. Urrutia said they harvested "old, big, yellow pine, five feet across, nice and clean. . . . We picked the best timber. Nothing like these poles they cut today," referring to the logs which the sawmills process nowadays.

He had a partner with a crosscut, two-man saw, an old timber-cutter some thirty years older than himself. His name was Leo Car, and he had lots of experience as a logger.

"He wanted me to give power on the saw, so he picked me up, to help him," says Urrutia.

Leo had a temper, however. One time they were un-

Ignacio Urrutia (in the middle) with his cousins Joe and Louie Epelde, Boise, Idaho, 1940.

dercutting and he got mad. He twisted the saw and one tooth caught Urrutia, cutting his wrist, from which he began to bleed profusely. There was no doctor in sight, and all he could do was to tie his handkerchief around the wound and keep working.

Leo was friendly and a good sawyer, and certainly the best saw sharpener. That guy could file a saw like a razor. Saw sharpening was a specialized skill and was performed only by experienced people. Urrutia never tried to learn it.

When the tree's diameter was too big around for the saw, they used springboards. With an axe they made a cut five feet above the ground and drove a large board into it by hitting it with the axe. The operation was repeated on the other side of the tree trunk. Once the boards were in place the two sawyers climbed up and stood on them. It was much more difficult than working from the ground, because you have to saw and balance yourself at the same time.

But that was not the worst of it. When the big tree began making cracking sounds and leaned, the sawyers had no time to waste; they hollered "timber," threw the saw down, jumped off the board, and started running as fast as they could. Sometimes it was downright dangerous, because one could not tell which way the tree would fall. Fortunately for Urrutia, he was a fast runner. They used to leave great big stumps in the forest and a lot of material was wasted, something they do not do today.

Logging became a lot harder when they were caught by an unexpected snowfall, which blanketed the ground. If the weather stayed cold, walking on it was easy, but when the sun softened the snow, the loggers sank and the job became a lot messier. Leo Car and Urrutia felled about twenty to thirty trees a day. After trimming the branches off, the logs were cut in thirty- to thirty-two-foot sections. Some trees were so large, clean, and straight that limb trimming was minimal.

Every morning, the foreman assigned each team their logging parameters. A logging crew numbered between twenty and forty people. The downed logs were dragged to the loading site by bulldozers and, when the terrain was too steep, by two horses. Cranes near the railroad loaded them onto thirty or forty flatcars, which is all the engine could handle down the mountain. The engineer took it very slowly, and he made sure that the train had good brakes.

An Unexpected Trip

One day when Urrutia was working at the logging camp the company had in New Meadows, a message came to the camp's main office. The year was 1939, when Europe was engulfed in World War II. About this time, too, fingerprinting was being implemented extensively in the United States. The telephone message said that the government wanted Urrutia's identification, and he had to present himself at the Boise State Capitol in such and such a room and on such and such a day. Urrutia was incredulous at first and asked the messenger if he was sure that it was he they wanted.

"Yes, they got your name, age, and everything. You are the one," he replied convincingly.

"Who's calling?" Urrutia asked.

"To tell you the truth, I think they want to send you back to Spain."

Urrutia was thoroughly scared. He had been eight years in the United States, but the thought of immigration officers, the FBI, and the police frightened him just the same. He had an old car at the camp, but he did not try to run away or anything. That same day, he drove straight to Boise, which was about seventy miles away, and went to his aunt's boardinghouse. He asked one of his cousins to accompany him to the State Capitol, which is next to Idaho Street. In fact, from the boardinghouse you could see the State Capitol.

On the arranged day, his youngest cousin, Louie Epelde, went with him to the State Capitol as interpreter. The room was upstairs and they went inside, where they found five officers, each one at his own desk. Pretty soon they saw they were not alone. Sixty-seven Basques were standing, some shaken, while others appeared pale. Urrutia looked at them and said to himself, "What is going on in here? I guess this was bound to happen." His cousin said in Basque, "Don't worry, I don't think they can do anything to you, but they will ask you a lot of questions."

Have You Been a Good Boy?

One of the officers called his name and pointing at a chair next to his desk asked him to sit down. He opened a book and began the inquiry:

"When did you leave the ship? What ship were you working on?"

"*Aldecoa*," Urrutia answered.

He saw the date written on the book. The government had it right. Urrutia still remembers the next questions, "Have you ever been married in this country? Did you ever make any girls pregnant?"

Urrutia understood both questions and responded in the negative.

"Well, that is what I wanted to know. If you tell me the truth, I want to let you go back to work," the agent said. Urrutia promised to tell the truth.

"Were you ever arrested in Spain? Do you have a criminal record in Spain?"

"No."

The officer said, "I will tell you what, we are going to send you back to your job. I will give you this card, and every month you are going to send the card to Washington, D.C., so we know whether you are still working in the same place or not."

Urrutia felt a great relief. As an added bonus, he was able to answer most questions himself, except for a couple which his cousin, who was right behind, helped him with. As instructed, and without wasting any time in Boise, he went right back to the logging camp. When he arrived, fellow workers wanted to know what the trip was all about, and he told them that they were not going to deport him after all. "I have some [of the] best records here and in the Old Country," he told them.

Urrutia was still mystified as to how the government had managed to find him. He had changed his name when he entered this country. How did they trace his footsteps to the wild country of Idaho? The police were probably well aware that most people who deserted a ship such as the *Aldecoa* registered in Bilbao went straight for Aguirre's hotel or other hotels patronized by Spanish nationals. They had the records from the *Aldecoa,* which they could compare with the hotel registry at Aguirre's. They also knew that from there, the worn-out trail led to one of the sheep towns in the West. Or, did the government have an informant among the Boise Basque community? Urrutia could only guess and wonder.

Because of his clean record and because he had been always employed, he was allowed to stay. Others were not so lucky. Three Basques who had police records in Spain were deported. Urrutia felt fairly safe now, since the law said that after five years in this country a person could not be deported. Of course, that did not mean an end to discrimination.

It was shortly after that time when the sixty-seven Basques with difficulties with the U.S. Immigration Office retained a lawyer from Boise, who was American, married to a Basque woman from Shoshone, Idaho. He told them that he wanted to take their case all the way to Washington, D.C. In fact, he was going to introduce a petition in Congress. Urrutia signed the papers and so did the rest. The lawyer, apparently on his own, flew to Washington several times, because he had to be present to introduce the bill. But the country was at war—FDR was president—and the bill was quickly brushed aside as soon as it was introduced. There were more pressing matters to deal with. The lawyer's interest was commendable, however, and we will return to this matter later.

Urrutia had the unrelenting ambition to learn English, and he took advantage of any available opportunity. He read the newspapers, even though often he did not understand what he was reading, and whenever he was in Boise he went to the show house. He did not like going to bars or poolhalls, which were smoke-filled. There were several show houses, and sometimes he went to three different shows in one day. Just by listening to people talk in the show and paying attention to the facial expressions, he was able to understand a lot. He recalled the early days at the logging camp when he could not understand the commands and the names of the tools. The situation with English in the United States was not an unfamiliar one to him, for he remembered the first weeks and months at primary school in Galdakao, when he did not understand Spanish. Now he vowed to learn English as soon as possible.

After returning from his trip to Boise, he worked at the logging camp for another season. In the meantime, the four-hundred-pound Austrian died, and a new manager took over the operations. For Urrutia, the camp was not the same anymore, and he began to look elsewhere for employment.

SEVEN

California Beginnings: 1940–1944

· · · · ·

Urrutia had been working eight years in Idaho, and he figured he had earned a little vacation. By then he owned a
1936 Chevrolet Coupe Master Deluxe with automatic trans-
mission, which he bought for $690 (cash, while earning
thirty-five cents an hour, he adds). In the company of two
of his Boise cousins, he headed south for Nevada.

They stopped in Las Vegas, which at the time was still a
dusty little town, not yet stormed by the Mob. They went
into a casino, and as they opened the door their eyes took a
few moments to adjust from the blazing sun outside to the
dimness of the casino. When finally their eyes were able to
distinguish the forms, they were jolted by the presence of a
guard with big whiskers and a pistol hanging from his hol-
ster belt. They did not like Las Vegas at all and went to sleep
in Boulder City.

From Vegas they traveled to Los Angeles. The Epelde
brothers wanted to visit the nightclubs in the city, and by
the time they left the last one, it was 2 A.M. They took a
look at their hotel in the distance, and they realized that it
would take a walk to reach it.

Not knowing which was the best route, Urrutia and his
cousins found themselves in a dark alley. Suddenly two
guys in dark clothes appeared coming toward them. As the
two men passed them, they began shouting "Hold it." As
soon as they heard the words, the three Idahoans thought

they said "holdup" and started running. In a flash, the long-legged Epelde brothers were gone, but Urrutia could not keep up with them. The two strangers caught up with the straggler, and when Urrutia began asking "what's going on" the men identified themselves as undercover cops.

"What are you doing here? Don't you know two people were murdered here a while ago?" they asked.

"We are not from here. We are vacationing," he told them.

In the meantime, his cousins, not waiting for him, had even crossed a canal with water up to their knees and had reached the top of the hill. Urrutia had quite a time catching up with them.

From Los Angeles they drove to San Francisco, where once again the two Epelde boys showed their love of acrobatics by jumping in and out of cable cars in motion. For Urrutia, the whole thing seemed like he was playing some sort of catch-up game.

From San Francisco they crossed the Sierra Nevada into Reno, where they visited the Bank Club casino. The two brothers started gambling at the dice table, one on each end, while Urrutia watched. He did not gamble. He did not like to *throw* his money away like that. One of the players at the table was from New York, and he was cleaning the house from the looks of the stack of chips in front of him. Urrutia recalls:

> Pretty soon, here was this guy putting his arm around one of my cousins. At first we didn't know and we thought nothing of it, but he was a queer! We left that place, and later as we were walking around in the street we saw the queer running out of the Bank Club casino with the police on his tail. That was a rough vacation.

All was quickly coming to an end, at least for Urrutia.

Ignacio Urrutia in Sacramento to enlist in the army, ca. 1942.

Loyalton, California: 1940–1942

Before leaving Reno, the Epelde boys remembered that a friend of theirs lived nearby in Loyalton, California, and they decided to pay a visit. She was Angela Bilbao, who was from Lekeitio, Bizkaia, and married to a man from Bilbao. She was Cruza Arostegui's sister, and for that reason the Epelde boys called her "aunt."[1]

Loyalton, located in the eastern foothills of the pine-forested Sierra, is about forty miles northwest of Reno. It was a little logging and ranching town with considerable sheep-herding activity during summer and fall. While they visited with their friends, Mr. Bilbao mentioned that there might be job openings in the lumber mill in town. Urrutia liked the idea and indicated his interest.

"I'll give you a job, and if you take it you can stay with us in the house. We got an extra room in here," the man said.

Trying to convince him, he added that it was a better deal than Idaho, working two seasonal jobs in the logging camps and in the sheep industry.

"Well, I'm staying then," Urrutia finally announced.

The three tourists had been traveling in Urrutia's car, so when his job in Loyalton was settled, he had no choice but to say good-bye to his cousins.[2] He took them back to Reno and put them on the bus to Boise.

"I don't think they were very happy with it. But to me it was an adventure," says Urrutia.

It is clear that he must have been ready to change jobs and his surroundings to see what other opportunities awaited him elsewhere. As Urrutia says, he did not enjoy the vacation too much, so this was a good way to end it. It seems that Urrutia was so full of energy that he always pre-ferred doing something to being idle.

He stayed in Loyalton for two years, working in the lum-ber mill. "Dry chain" was his job, that is, sorting lumber by size as it comes out of the planer. The United States was gearing up for World War II, and all the output of the mill had been contracted by the government. While doing gov-ernment work, the mill was subject to government rules. Thus, one morning Urrutia went to work as usual at eight A.M., and the foreman in his department called him over, "I want to talk to you." Urrutia was thinking, "Oh, oh. In two years he never said a word to me, and now he calls me. I think something is cooking."

"Are you an American citizen?" he asked.

"No."

"Do you have your first papers, where your entry into this country is documented?"

"No. I don't have any papers."

"Are you illegal in this country?"

"Yes."[3]

"I'm sorry. I received a notice from the union that you must be fired, because you are dangerous. You're a fifth-column communist, and you plan to blow up the mill."

"I do not know what you're talking about," Urrutia said.

"Well, you see that office over there across the street?"

"Yes."

"You go over there, and the check will be ready for you."

Urrutia went to the office. In two years he had not been there once. He saw a check on top of the desk and asked if it was his check, but nobody answered. Nobody would talk to him. So he grabbed the check and left. He didn't think that was very nice. He summed up his feelings on the matter:

I was working hard every day and producing everything for the government. I went to the union meetings—you had to go or they fined you five dollars. One day during the meeting, somebody next to me got up and said, "Mr. President, first thing we have to do is throw these aliens out of the country. They are dangerous." I looked at him but thought, "I'd better keep it quiet." He was a big man. The president answered the man, "Well, I don't know if we can do that. We have a lot of aliens working here. They get low wages in the mill. If we fire all of them, we're going to lose this contract." And I was thinking, "Well, you gave a good answer for this gentleman next to me." I thought it was kind of rude what he was proposing.

Rude or not, Urrutia was thrown out of the mill, and no other alien suffered his fate. Once again, he found himself with nothing, and that made him want something even more.

Susanville Beginnings

It was 1942, and Urrutia had no choice but leave the town of Loyalton. About fifty miles north as the crow flies is Susanville, California, and on the same day of his dismissal Urrutia decided to try his search for another job there. He always seemed to be rather lucky finding employment. He landed at the Fruitgrowers Supply Company and inquired about his chances of getting a job.

"Sure, you can come to work tomorrow, or today, right now, if you want to," was the answer.

"Are you union?" asked Urrutia.

"No, we don't have union."

"Well, in that case I will start working, but if you belong to a union, I don't want to work for you guys."

"No, no, we are not union. You can just come in and go to work."

According to a report that appeared in a Susanville paper fifty-four years later, Urrutia obtained the job at Fruit-growers at midnight on the same day that he had been fired from Loyalton.[4] He was the kind of man who could not stand being without a job.

He stayed at Fruitgrowers until 1944. The mill cut timber in the national forest and employed over two hundred women who made boxes for the fruit growers in California. Urrutia worked in the green lumberyard. It was hard work, but he did not hold back and worked diligently. Still, his heart was elsewhere, in shop-keeping, and that is why he obtained a part-time job in a small grocery store.

Uncle Sam Does Not Want Me

In 1942 he was badly shaken by the Loyalton experience. He reasoned that if it had happened to him eight years earlier, in Idaho, when he was a total stranger in this country, he would have understood it, but now? After so many years and after he knew the citizenship book by heart? He thought it was unfair, and he decided to do something about it.

Urrutia went to Sacramento, California, and signed up as a volunteer to the U.S. Army. He took the physical and did not pass. He passed the strictly physical part, but he was classified 4-F or illiterate. They gave him a test book with marks. "I knew where the marks went but the hell with it," he said, and that cost him. Thus, a man who could not only read and write English but knew accounting and spoke three languages, a man who had taught citizenship classes, was classified as illiterate.

"We will call you," he was told.

The doctor who examined him consoled him. "Don't worry, they will call you pretty soon. You have to go to school, and from there they will take you to the army."

He returned to Susanville encouraged. He had a new job, and he was working hard at it. He read the local paper all the time to stay informed of developments regarding the school for people like himself. As it turned out, there were too many illiterates taking such classes. He did not learn anything and sometimes the teacher did not even show up, but he had to attend in order to prove that he had been in class. In the end, they never called him from the school or from the army. Not that he was eager to fight and kill people, no, not particularly. He wanted the citizenship pa-

The personnel at the Royal Grocery, Susanville, California, 1949. Left to right: Ed Young, Clyde Bowles, Lloyd Wood, Don Stokes, Monty Bates, unidentified clerk, unidentified female (bookkeeper), and Ignacio Urrutia, who managed the store.

pers so that he would not be kicked around and fired from jobs.

Meanwhile, there were some developments on another front.

Proud Citizen: 1944

The bill that the Idaho lawyer had introduced in Congress in 1940 on behalf of sixty-seven Basques was finally signed by President Franklin D. Roosevelt in 1943. It allowed them to remain in the United States and, if they wanted to, become citizens. The only thing they had to pay was an entry tax of $10 or $12.

Urrutia saw his name and the names of the sixty-six

compatriots in the *San Francisco Examiner*. To this day, he is sorry that he did not clip and save the page. For him that was the greatest news: now he could become a citizen. He called the lawyer in Boise and authorized him to start the application proceedings for his citizenship.

In 1944 he filed his application papers for citizenship in Susanville, and at night he took classes at the high school.

"You had to go to school; it was hard if you did not go to school," he says, even though he already knew a great deal.

When the scheduled day to get his papers arrived, he was called to appear in court. It was 1944. He was sitting where the jury sits. About thirty people were going to be given citizenship certificates, and the room was full of people; some were family or friends, others just curious about who was becoming a citizen. As he sat down, Urrutia noticed that the judge was looking at him and observing him. It made him nervous.

Finally, it was Urrutia's turn to be examined on his knowledge of English and other matters concerning the United States government and the Constitution. The examiner kept asking him questions, and he kept answering every one of them, because he had memorized the book in Idaho. It was a very easy exam, except one question about Alaska, which was not in the book he had studied, because he said it had been printed before Alaska was purchased from Russia. When the exam concluded, the judge, Ben Curl, said to him, "You still cannot become an American citizen, because you should be fighting for your country."

Urrutia did not say anything, and the examiner requested the judge's permission to ask Urrutia a question. The judge motioned him to go ahead, and the examiner queried Urrutia, "[Do] you have a draft card or anything that [indicates] you have gone to the army, that you tried to enlist?"

"Yes, I have a draft card. I got it two years ago," Urrutia answered as he handed it to him.

The examiner, after looking at the card, addressed the judge, "Well, this man volunteered for the U.S. Army, and he did not pass for illiteracy. I think he has done his duty."

The judge said, "We have to ask him if he can read the paper."

So they brought a copy of the *Lassen Advocate* to him. Urrutia remembers vividly:

> I had already read what was in that paper, so they gave me this old paper with the Office of Price Administration rules, and I read it, and they wanted to know if I understood it, so I explained the whole thing.

Then the judge requested that he read another paragraph written in little black letters. It was a story about the Red Cross. He read that, too, and the judge wanted to know what it said.

"Well, it says that the Red Cross is coming . . . they want to collect so many thousands of dollars by such and such date."

Now the examiner intervened, "Your Honor, this man knows the Constitution of the United States better than you and I. He can read, and he understands what he is reading. In two years this fellow made great progress, and I do not think you can stop him from becoming an American citizen."

The judge agreed and said, "Pass."

Urrutia returned to his seat and thought he was going to pass out, he was so excited! There were some Basques and some Italians in the crowd of prospective recipients of citizenship, but Urrutia does not remember if they passed or failed. He does remember what happened to the next candidate who was examined after him, an older fellow. The examiner asked him a question, and he didn't answer it; he asked him another, and the same thing happened. Three questions and no answer. And the judge said, "Pass." The examiner objected, "Your Honor, this gentleman did not answer the questions on the Constitution. Now, I want to know if he can read. Because you made this man here [Urrutia] answer all the questions in the book, and then you made him read. So, before this gentleman can pass, let us see if he can read."

They gave the man the same old newspaper, and he could not read it. The examiner said, "Your Honor, we've got to stay within the rules. This man does not know the Constitution of the United States, and there is no way he can pass and become American citizen if he cannot read or does not understand."

None of the four people tested after Urrutia passed. After the ceremony, they approached him, and one of them said in an accusatory tone of voice, "We think this is all your fault."

"No. That's your good friend, the judge," Urrutia replied [because the judge knew them].

They may have been overconfident, Urrutia thinks. He himself did not know the judge at all. When he went to get his citizenship papers, that was the first time that he saw him. A few days later, when he was working at the grocery store, Ben Curl walked into the store and, seeing Urrutia, said, "Hello."

"Hello," Urrutia answered.

That was the first time he had seen him come to the store. Still, Urrutia had not changed his mind about the exam day, when the judge was rude to him simply because he was not serving the country. The judge did not know that he had done his best, that he had volunteered. And after one volunteered, automatically one was entitled to citizenship, whether he could read or not. Still, Urrutia holds no grudges. "That was the happiest day of my life, when I got my citizenship papers. Because in those days you could not even get a job if you were not a citizen, it was hard to get jobs. So when the U.S. Army refused to take me, I had to get the papers another way, on my own."

Even today, strong emotions overtake Urrutia whenever he recalls that day in court. He can hardly contain his exuberance, and again he says:

I was the happiest man alive in the country. I was living scared, scared in every place I worked, scared that somebody might seize me and take me out of the country. Since then I can do a lot of things for the country, I can go into business—like I had planned to do—if I stayed in this country. So, in 1944 I got my citizenship papers.

Two Incidents

Since 1942 Urrutia had been working at the Fruitgrowers lumber mill from 8 A.M. to 5 P.M. Afterward, he went to work as a clerk in a little grocery store until 10 P.M. "See, grocery business was in my blood. I wanted to get in there and give my English a little practice," he says. Lowell Hardy, owner of the Economic Groceries, said to him, "I'll give you a steady job if you want to work."

"Yes. I would like to work here. That's my ambition, to work in a grocery store."

By that time, Urrutia could speak English pretty well, and he was getting better at it all the time. Lowell Hardy showed him how to use the telephone to order merchandise and other such duties. Pretty soon, he started calling Sacramento and other places. By nature he was sort of bashful and never too forward talking to people, but he was getting used to it and to the telephone as well. Hardy was encouraging: "You don't have any problem. You just go and do it."

"In that case, I'll do it," Urrutia said eagerly.

And he did. "I wasn't shy in the store." He was charged up and in charge. He had the key to the place, too.

So now he had two jobs, and he kept them for two years. Everything was going fairly well until one September day in 1944. It was Labor Day, and Miguel Petralanda, a Bizkaian friend from Galdakao, came to town for a visit. He was a navy man on an American warship that had been hit by the Japanese and was docked in Portland, Oregon, for repairs. Urrutia had been working hard for Mr. Hardy for nearly two years, so he figured that he would take some time off to be with his friend. He asked if at least he could have Labor Day off, and Hardy said, "That is our biggest day. Everybody else in town is closed, and I want you to stay here because there will be a lot of customers." Urrutia pleaded, "Can't you do the job for me? I have a friend coming from a warship, and he is pretty well shook up. I want to spend some time with him."

"I'm sorry. I have to have you in the store tomorrow," he insisted.

Urrutia was ticked off then. He replied, "In that case, I don't need your job. The guy is fighting for the country, and he is coming to see me. I think I should spend some time with him."

Urrutia quit the job and gave his boss an additional reason why he did not want to work for him anymore. He said, "Do you remember when they arrested me for selling beer to a person who was in the U.S. Navy, a twenty-year-old man? Well, at the time I did not know the laws of the country or that you're supposed to be twenty-one to drink." (It was easy to understand why Urrutia would be oblivious to liquor laws; he had spent all his years in the United States in sheep and logging camps, and when he had a drink in town it was probably in one of the Basque boardinghouses.)

This is how the incident with the beer had occurred: The navy man came in to buy two cases of beer, and Urrutia saw him waiting to pay for it at the check-out stand. The owner, though in the store, was not attending the young man, so Urrutia went over to the cash register and asked the owner for the price of the beer, and the owner told him how much to charge the young man.

The next day, Urrutia was working in the mill when the police came in and arrested him.

"We are taking you to jail," the police said. Urrutia wanted to know why, and so did the boss at the mill.

"I wouldn't know why they are taking me. I didn't do anything. I didn't kill anybody. I'm an honest man, but if they want to take me, let them," was Urrutia's answer.

The police took him to jail and showed him the cell where the navy guy, still in uniform, was. Urrutia recognized him. He had taken the beer behind the high school, and a lot of minors had been drinking with him. The police said, "Didn't you know that according to the law you have to be twenty-one to buy liquor?"

"No, I didn't know, but the owner of the store should have, because he was there. It was he who told me what the price of the beer was. He should have told me I couldn't sell it to him. I did what my boss told me."

Then they took Urrutia to another room, where the officer in charge of the liquor control was waiting for him.

"You sold liquor to a minor. That is a criminal offense."

"I understand what criminal means. I don't think I killed anybody.[5] Did my legs and arms take the beer behind the school?

"Maybe I'm guilty, but I didn't do anything that I knew was wrong. But if that's the way the law reads. . ."

"Yes, you're a criminal in this country. You broke the law."

"I'm sorry," Urrutia replied.

The following week, Urrutia appeared in court. The store owner was present as well, and he advised him to plead guilty and pay the fine. So when the judge asked him, "How do you plead?" the owner nodded and Urrutia pleaded guilty. He was fined $500, and he paid the fine because he did not want to go to jail for six months, which was the alternative. Afterward, the owner approached him to say that he could return to work for him until the end of the year so that he could pay the fine, but Urrutia was not that kind of person:

> I don't want to work where there is danger. I don't want to be arrested. I don't know the laws, therefore, I don't think I should work there. I want to be free. They arrested me for something that I didn't even know why, and now you tell me to work for you for the rest of the year? I don't like that.

After the incident, Urrutia was not happy at the Economic Groceries. In fact, he went to see a lawyer, because he believed that he had been accused and fined unjustly. The lawyer—he may have been Hardy's lawyer as well, Urrutia quips—asked him just two questions:
"Did you sell the beer?"
"Yes."
"Did you take the money?"
"Yes."
"Then, it was your fault."
That cost him another $20. "Crooks! Those days!" he says with a dismissing gesture. It is no wonder that he quit on the day before Labor Day, just like that.

Urrutia also spoke about something else that happened to him in 1945 in Susanville. It was a good example of how a combination of factors allowed certain people to take advantage of minorities and immigrants.

One day, on a street near the river, Urrutia brought his

car to a halt and parked it on the right side of the road when another driver coming from the left crashed into it, causing considerable damage to the car. The sheriff came to the scene and after surveying the accident said to Urrutia, "I know that [other] fellow. I want to see your driver's license."

Urrutia gave it to him but was incensed by the fact that the sheriff showed no interest in the other driver, a young male who was slumped drunk at the wheel.[6] The sheriff recognized him as a recipient of public assistance. A few minutes later, the drunk man's sister showed up. She owned a bar in town and said to Urrutia, "Idaho, you go ahead and fix the car, and I will pay for the damages."

Urrutia believed her word, and the incident did not go any further. He now believes that she may have tipped the sheriff, who did not give the man a ticket for driving while intoxicated, nor did he write a report of the accident.

Because of World War II, car repairs were not allowed, so Urrutia had to wait about a year for the parts. Finally, when the car was fixed, he took the bill to the woman at the bar. She was accompanied by her lawyer, who told Urrutia, "I am sorry, but you are not going to get a penny out of this."

"Why not? She told me that she would pay," Urrutia replied, looking at the woman, who kept her lips very tight.

The lawyer said, "You don't have anything written. You have no record."

For Urrutia, a person's word was a good enough record. In fact, in Argentina they have an expression, *palabra de vasco* (word of a Basque), which is a better guarantee than a written document.

On a glorious spring day of 1999, reminiscing about that 1945 accident, Urrutia was still disgusted, but concluded philosophically, "I had to pay the bill, which was thousands of dollars. A lot of money in those days."

EIGHT

Working for Royal Grocery: 1944–1966

· · · · ·

The next day after quitting at Economic Groceries—it was September 1944—Urrutia was walking down Main Street in Susanville and a fellow told him of a new store that had just opened. Urrutia thanked him and went over to see the place. He found two partners opening the business. Royal Stewart was a grocer and William Crabbe was a butcher. One of them said to him, "If you want to come to work for us, you can try one week. I'll give you $50. If you don't like it, you go back wherever you come from."

"I'll take it," Urrutia replied.

That was the beginning of a twenty-two-year relationship with Royal Grocery. At the beginning, as in any new business, there was not much going on. They were remodeling, too, and it was a slow start for Royal Grocery, but hard work, as Urrutia would say, proved itself (i.e., yielded results). Eventually, the manager, Royal Stewart, was pretty happy because business was getting better and better. The partners were young, and they worked hard. Urrutia was their age, and he worked as hard as they, often seven days a week.

It was a great venture. Urrutia gave his best, and the owners appreciated that. To quote from an account that appeared in the *Lassen Advocate* in 1980 about his years at the Royal Grocery:

Sixteen to twenty-hour days were not strangers. . . .
Idaho is in the store by 4 A.M. every day—allowing

Ignacio Urrutia leaving the TWA plane in Barajas airport, Madrid, Spain, 1950. He does not know who took this picture, which was mailed to him in Galdakao a few days later. It was his first trip back home.

himself time to work on the books until opening the doors at about 5 A.M. Through the day he can be found working behind the meat counter, putting out produce, marking cans, working at the cash register or chatting with the scores of acquaintances he has made through the years.[1]

The Visit Home: 1950

Urrutia had worked for Royal for six years without taking a vacation, and in 1950 the owners decided that he deserved one. They informed him that the firm was sending him to Europe for a visit to see his mother, and "when you return, maybe you will work just as hard or better for us," they said. Furthermore, Royal gave him a letter for his mother, written in English, which Urrutia had to translate. It said that the reason why they were sending him home was because of his performance on the job. In other words, that he had earned the vacation.

Ignacio Urrutia's first visit home. Left to right: Ignacio Urrutia, Petra Urrutia, and Josemari Diego, Galdakao, Bizkaia, 1950.

Urrutia accepted the offer from his employers, because now he was a American citizen and could travel abroad and return to the United States. Earlier, he could not. "That was very nice. I worked very hard for them, and they returned the favor . . . that was the first time in nineteen years that I went to see my mother," Urrutia says. He had an American passport and a visa to enter Spain. Furthermore, the Spanish consul in San Francisco wrote a little note on his behalf stating that they could not bother him for the time he was in Spain. One reason for the note was that when Urrutia

Urrutia with his half-brothers and sisters while vacationing in Bizkaia in 1950. Back left to right: Encarna Diego, Maria Diego (a stepsister), Lolita Diego, Manolita Diego, and Maria Carmen Diego. Front left to right: Ignacio Urrutia and Jesus Diego.

jumped ship, he was technically classified as a deserter from the Spanish navy.[2]

He received a paid one-month vacation, which was an honorable thing for a small company like Royal to do. But Urrutia had demonstrated ample loyalty, and he had put in a lot of time. "I worked with them just like if they were brothers. I was taking care of their business," Urrutia sums it up.

Crossing New York City

He flew to New York and from New York to Madrid, round-trip. When the plane landed in New York, he had to

Left: Uncle Martin Urrutia, an ex-sheepherder, who supported Ignacio's plan to go into the merchant marine. Ignacio Urrutia (fifth from left) is surrounded by relatives on his mother's side, 1950.

Ignacio Urrutia (kneeling with dog) and his mother's family in Galdakao, Bizkaia, 1950.

wait all night for a connection to Madrid. All he could do was to sit at the airport and wait. He was practically alone. He saw several well-dressed white men at a distance, and one of them approached him to inform him that his plane was not coming any time soon and wondered if he wanted

Left to right: Ignacio Urrutia, Julian Moreno, Maria, Manolita, Encarna, Itziar, Jose Doistua, Jesus Diego, Mari Bego, and Petra Urrutia, Bizkaia, 1957.

Marceline Gastanaga in Baiona, ca. 1946.

to go up to the control tower to look around. Urrutia agreed, and the two of them went into an elevator, which started ascending, but pretty soon it stopped. In the blinking of an eye, before Urrutia knew what hit him, he realized that his pants were down. Recovering from the shock, he grabbed at his pants and quickly pulled them back up. Now in a rage, he turned to the stranger and said, "If you don't put this elevator down, I will kill you, I will choke you right now."

"OK, OK," the man said, and he turned the elevator back on and began descending.

Still incensed, Urrutia got out of the elevator and returned to the waiting area. He was dumbfounded at the incident. He had never heard of any such behavior in the places he had lived before. "I didn't notice anything; that's how fast he pulled my pants down." His 1932 stay in New York had been a pleasant one, but this experience now put a bad taste in his mouth.

After enjoying the month with his family in Bizkaia, it was time to say good-bye to his mother and return to the United States. His mother wanted to send him off with something special, and she had prepared homemade *txorizos* (Basque sausages), not the fresh kind, but the smoked and dried ones, which are better. She wrapped about ten pounds of sausages and put them in a box for her son.

The plane from Madrid landed Urrutia in New York once again, and he headed for the customs counter. As he faced the officer—a large black man—he put the sausage box on top of the counter. The officer took a whiff and said, "Oh, my God, what is this?" Urrutia told him. The officer grabbed the box and went into a back room. Urrutia waited and waited, and there was no sign of his *txorizo* box or the black man, so he turned to the next customs officer and asked why the man was not returning.

"What did you have in the box?" he inquired.

"Ten pounds of homemade sausages."

"Oh, if he smelled those *txorizos,* you will never see him again. He took them home."

"You mean he took home the *txorizos my* mother made *for me?*" he asked in disbelief.

"Yes."

Urrutia was livid. "You know, I have never seen too many blacks in my life, but this guy makes me want to hate them all."

Urrutia was not aware that bringing meat into the United States was illegal. He says, "If I had known that, I would have thrown the *txorizos* out of the plane into the sea for the fishes."

After those two unfortunate incidents in New York City, he returned to Susanville and to Royal Grocery. "Those were years of prosperity. You worked and you produced. In those days, we were making money, but we worked hard and everybody was working and the money kept coming," says Urrutia.

After several years, the two original partners split up. Crabbe opened his own store in Herlong, California, about thirty miles south of Susanville, and Stewart remained the sole owner in Susanville. In addition, Royal had trucks that transported lumber down the valley and brought groceries and vegetables back to Susanville. The store in Susanville also sold appliances and televisions. Business was prospering in the post–World War II years and in the 1950s.

Marriage and Family

Urrutia met his future wife, Marceline Gastanaga, at the grocery store in Susanville, where he was working. In the 1920s and 1930s, many Basque women came to work in the *ostatuak* or boardinghouses of the American West as maids and as hired help. Marceline came in 1949 to work for the

Left to right: Marceline Urrutia and her daughter, Mary Jane, standing next to Urrutia's 1955 Cadillac, behind the Royal Grocery store, Herlong, California, 1956.

St. Francis Hotel in Susanville, where she had acquaintances. She was born on January 20, 1928, at the farmstead Saleria in Esterenzubi, a town in Iparralde (French Basque Country). Many other emigrants from her hometown came to the United States to work in the sheep industry. Soon after she arrived, she was married to Jean Pierre Sarry from Baigorry. The couple had a daughter, Mary Jane (Harriet), and divorced a year or two later.

One day in 1954, Marceline came to Royal Grocery to

Left to right: Ignacio Urrutia, his wife, Marceline, and her daughter, Mary Jane, Susanville, California, ca. 1955.

Left to right: Marceline (holding Reneé), Mary Jane, and Ignacio (holding Joey), ca. 1960.

Left to right: Marceline, Mary Jane, Robert, Ignacio, Michel Iribarren, and Pete Gotari, an ex-sheepherder. Front left to right: Joey and Reneé, ca. 1968.

shop, where she was introduced to Urrutia. A year later they were married in Reno.[3] They produced three children: Reneé (Jones), Joey, and Robert. The Urrutias built a home in Susanville in 1956, where they had a wonderful and happy life together.

Urrutia of course raised Marceline's daughter as well. In a telephone conversation with Mary Jane in June 1999, she said that for all practical purposes, Mr. Idaho is her father. "He raised me," she added. She recalls that when she started kindergarten she only spoke Basque, and she didn't know how to pray in English until she went to church for catechism. As is typical in immigrant families, Mary Jane taught English to her sister Reneé, who was bilingual when she started kindergarten. By age twelve, Mary Jane was writing checks for the household expenses, and Urrutia would sign them.

The Grocery Store Beat: 1966–1968

Urrutia worked at Royal Grocery until 1966, but some time before that he was made a partner in the business. He did not like the partnership and quit working at Royal altogether. He went to see a lawyer in Reno, but all he got for his share of the partnership was $1,000, which barely paid the lawyer's fees. Before long, the store went bankrupt and the place was closed.

After twenty-two years of employment stability, a period of job changes and relative insecurity followed, but not unemployment. That word did not exist in Urrutia's vocabulary. In 1966, on the same day he was hired by Miller Market, he had another job offer as well, from Rusty Market. Miller's was closer, so he took it. At the same time, on a part-time basis, he also worked at the Paul Bunyan Mill. Soon after he started working for Miller's Market, the store hired another man who was deeply in debt and needed money desperately. They hired the man and reduced Urrutia's hours to just two days a week. He did not think that was fair, and he complained to the union, who said they could do nothing about it.

Now Urrutia had five days off, and being a person who could not sit still very long (although during his train trip from New York to Boise he managed to remain seated for three straight days), he drove his truck to Chico, California, loaded it with fruits and vegetables, returned to Susanville, and peddled them to small businesses and house-to-house. He needed a place to store the excess merchandise, so he built a cooler attached to his garage. Those were sixteen-hour days, but for Urrutia it was part of his adventure. Anything was better than being idle.

Miller's Market filed suit against him because he was undercutting his employer, but the union ruled in Urrutia's favor. Meanwhile, the main office advised Miller to fire Urrutia. The latter, angered by the decision, took off his apron and threw it in his employer's face.

"No, no, put the apron back on," the manager said.

"Hell, no. If the main office told you to fire me, I am gone," Urrutia replied.

The manager became upset and walked across the street to Walker's Café for a cup of coffee, and during the conversation he mentioned the incident with Urrutia. Later that day, Jim Walker, the owner of the Café, saw Urrutia and said to him, "Hey, Idaho, I heard they fired you, or you quit. So come work for me. I will pay you more, and you can sell all the produce you want, to me included."

Such was Urrutia's uncanny luck. He always seemed to get jobs in the nick of time. He worked at Walker's for three months, until one day, the fellow from Sacramento who owned the Royal Grocery store dropped by for coffee and found Urrutia flipping hamburgers.

"Idaho, what are you doing here? You are a grocery man, not a restaurant man."

"I do anything. See these hamburgers?" Urrutia replied.

That night, the man came to visit Urrutia at home and asked him to take over the grocery store, but he refused. Urrutia explains the situation:

> In 1966, before declaring bankruptcy, if Royal had let me have the grocery store, I could have made the payments. I could have made it easy. But he had a drinking problem, and he liquidated everything in the store. He didn't have to. The store was doing OK.

For the moment, Urrutia was not going to jump at the chance to be in business. However, the man was right; Urrutia's heart was not in a restaurant, and as soon as he had an offer from a grocery store, he quit Walker's Café. It was 1967 when he started working for Hills Market.

There were several small grocery stores in Susanville, and in 1968 he began working for Washoe Market as well. "This guy at the Washoe Market needed help, anyway," Urrutia explains. He was hired as an assistant manager, but the job did not last very long because the place was bought out by Eagle Thrifty of Reno. Ten days later, all the employees at Washoe Market lost their jobs. "Eagle Thrifty bought the business, but they did not buy the help," says Urrutia.

After Urrutia was laid off, he tried to be rehired by Eagle Thrifty, but this time his earlier luck had run out. They had a new manager there, and even though he kept knocking on his door every day for three weeks, the answer was always the same, "Sorry, we don't need anybody today."

Yet the manager was hiring people, so Urrutia was wondering what was going on. He decided to go to Reno to the main office of Eagle Thrifty to meet with the owner of the company, Jose Gastanaga, a fellow Basque.[4] When he entered the office, a man there asked him, "Are you having a meeting [appointment] with him?"

"No, I come in to talk."

"Sorry, you need to make an appointment," he said.

Just then, the former owner of Washoe Market happened to walk into the office and said, "Idaho, what are you doing here? Aren't you working in Susanville?"

"No, these guys took it over and they won't hire me back."

"Oh, don't worry, they will put you back."

"It's been three weeks so far, and they hired all new people and they never put me back."

"I'll talk to Mr. Gastanaga," he said.

As he finished the sentence, Gastanaga was walking out of the door, and he heard the noise. Urrutia went over to him. "Mr. Gastanaga, my name is Ignacio Urrutia. I came in to see what's going on in Susanville. They won't hire me."

"I have managers down there taking care of that end of the business, so you have to talk to them. I don't do the hiring, they do."

The former owner of Washoe Market said reassuringly, "Don't worry, they'll put you in there."

He returned to Susanville, and the following day he was going to give Eagle Thrifty another try, but before leaving home he said to his wife Marceline, "This is my last visit. If I don't get a job today, I am not knocking on that door anymore."

Urrutia felt sort of humiliated that after forty years in this country he had to try so hard to get a job that he knew he could do better than many others hired at Eagle Thrifty. Marceline replied, "What are you going to do?"

"Something, but I won't starve," he answered.

On that day, he got the job. There was another manager at the store who had been sent by Reno Eagle Thrifty. "Are you Idaho?" he asked.

"Yes."

"Get your apron."

"Ah, well, thank God, today was going to be the last day I would come here asking for a job."

"Really?"

"Yes, the other manager wouldn't hire me."

"Well, you got the job. We received a good recommendation out of Reno on your behalf. So, just get your apron."

He went to work on the floor of Eagle Thrifty. They offered him a spot at the check-out, but he did not accept it, preferring to handle the floor. They asked him a number of questions, such as how many years he had worked for Royal Grocery. Then they dared ask him how much money he made, and Urrutia could not resist that one. He asked a question of his own to one of the interviewers. "Are you guys with the FBI? Because I don't think it is any of your business to ask me how much money I was making working for somebody else. If you ask me how much money I want to make working for you, then fine."

The interviewer was apparently impressed with Urrutia's straightforward response and made a remark to the manager concerning his smarts.

"I might be smart, but nobody is going to tell me what I do in my business. I don't ask you what you do in your business," Urrutia told them.

He was frank, blunt even, with them, but they hired him anyway. During the three months he was with Eagle Thrifty, he worked harder than some other people he saw walking back and forth in the store with a cup of coffee in their hand.

"Without any cup of coffee or glass of water, I worked my eight hours. I sweated and showed those guys what kind of work I did," says Urrutia with pride, but still feeling a bit hurt that they did not want to hire him.

NINE

Idaho Grocery: July 1, 1968

· · · · ·

All along, as he worked for the various grocery stores in Susanville, Urrutia was acquiring experience and valuable know-how in running a business. Perhaps as important was the fact that he came into contact with a lot of the people in town, whom he knew on a first-name basis. At the same time, he nurtured the dream of some day owning his own business, his own store, and that dream began to take shape in the summer of 1968.

He had been working a few months for Eagle Thrifty, when one day Roy Lazard, a contractor, approached him with a business proposition. Lazard had bought the Royal Grocery building in a bankruptcy court in Eureka, California. His wife was working for a title company, and he probably had inside information about the upcoming sale. He bought it before it was advertised. When Lazard came for a visit, Urrutia was at work at Eagle Thrifty, and he told him that he did not want to discuss business on the job. He asked Lazard to come to his home later on, and that same day he did so.

"You want to lease the place where you used to work? I bought the building, and if you want to open a grocery store, I will give you a good five-year lease on it," Lazard said.

"Well, I don't have any money to start a business," Urrutia replied.

"You can borrow it. Somebody will loan you the money

to start, and I'll tell you what I'll do. I'll give you a chance. I'll fix the building, and as a deposit you pay me the first and the last month, that's $1,000, and then $500 a month. I believe you can make that place go," he said.

"I can make the place go if I had something to sell, but I don't, and I don't have money to buy merchandise."

"Go see the banker. I think you can do good business, because you worked quite a few years in that place and you know a lot of people in this town," Lazard pointed out.

"Yes, I know a lot of people. And I am not worried about failing, but I don't have anything to start with."

"Well, you think it over," Lazard suggested.

That evening, Urrutia discussed the idea with Marceline, his wife, who suggested, "You can't lose anything. We don't have anything. You might as well go for it. You're working right now. You work hard, and you have nothing. If you work for yourself, you'll work hard and maybe you'll end up with something some day."

Marceline's reasoning was to the point, and suddenly Urrutia realized that having nothing all these years had been the powerful force that had spurred him on in his search for something better. It had been quite an adventure, but now it was clear that the time had come to grab at the opportunity of a lifetime. He signed the lease on July 1, 1968. He could not call it a store yet, because there was nothing in it.

"I Have Nothing To Sell"

"I started with nothing," Urrutia recalls. But nothing was precisely the power that had kept him going until, finally, he arrived. Now he had the business he had wanted ever since he was hired as a kitchen helper on the ship in England. He had come to the United States with the intention to start a business, and now that he had one, he realized he desperately needed something else—money. He went to his bank, and they told him that Susanville already had too many grocery stores, and besides, he owed too much money on his house loan.

"I owe you guys $13,000, and I am asking you for $10,000 more."

"We will have a meeting, and we will let you know," the banker told him.

Urrutia thanked him and left, and a few days later he learned that his application was turned down. So he went to the other bank, UCB Bank, and presented his business plans in a straightforward manner. UCB offered him a $2,000 loan payable in six months, and Urrutia took it.

> With the $2,000 I paid the rent for the first and last month, and I had a little money left, not very much, and I went there and started cleaning the place up. My beginning inventory was a gallon of milk, a loaf of bread, a carton of cigarettes, and a case of Coke. Everybody peeked through the window and asked, "What are you doing in here, Idaho?"

"Well, I don't know, but some day I might have a grocery store. If you guys help me I might be able to sell you some merchandise someday."

His biggest problem was not having the cash he needed to buy merchandise. He could not get it, and nobody gave him any credit. He called Red Bluff, where a friend of his owned an orchard. His name was Bill Kemp. His father and Urrutia had been coworkers at Paul Bunyan in Susanville, and they knew each other pretty well.

"What's happening?" Bill asked.

"I started in business and I don't have anything to sell."

"I can send you a load of peaches. You can pay me whenever you want."

"Why don't you send me five hundred boxes?" said the Basque prudently.

"I will send a truckload," Kent offered.

So he sent me a truckload of peaches, and I put them on the sidewalk outside the store, all stacked up from one end to another, and I announced the sale on the radio, "Peaches for sale at 2120 Main Street." In those days, it was $1.98 for a box of beautiful peaches. Those were the days. People came and I sold all the peaches, and with the money I bought more merchandise. I called Kemp to send me another load, so he did, and I sold them all as fast as they came in. They were canning peaches, and the price was reasonable . . . besides, I knew a lot of people in town. So I had a little money to start bringing to the store a few more things.

Stocking the Store

But Urrutia knew that if he really wanted to make it in the business, he had to have a full range of groceries and merchandise to sell. That is when he decided to go to Reno and talk to one of the wholesalers.

I went to Sun Blest Company. I knew the manager because my boss at the Royal Grocery bought a lot of merchandise from them. I went to the office and talked to them about my plans to go into business and how I wanted to have some groceries if they gave me an open account. I told them I could pay back two–three months later.

And the manager said to me, "I think we can trust you, you bought a lot of groceries from us, you sold a lot of groceries in Susanville. I will tell you what, I will give you $5,000 worth of groceries, and you pay us in six months, on your own terms."

So they brought me the groceries, and I put a little stack in here, a little stack there, and pretty soon it looked like I had a few groceries. Soon I started buying a little meat—you have to have a little meat. At the time, a nephew came from France, my wife's nephew. His name was Michel Iribarren. I had met him when he was seventeen, when he asked me, "*Otto* [uncle], when are you going to take me to America?" I answered him, "When you grow a little." We had a lawyer prepare the visa papers and he came. When I saw him, I said to him, "Well, you didn't grow very much." But anyway, we sent him to Ohio to a butcher school for three months to get a diploma. He returned and started working in the store, but without drawing any wages. They were lean years. We ate whatever little there was left in there, and we just worked. After Michel took over the butcher shop, we started going to the ranches, bringing in the beef to custom cut and wrap. And that is how the money was coming into the business. We did not have to buy the beef, just cut it and freeze it. So we were coming up.

Another person that helped us was Bob Pasero of Lassen Beverage. We had a license for beer and wine but could not offer any, because we lacked the money to buy the merchandise. So one day Pasero came in and said, "I will give you any quantity you want, to pay back whenever you can." It was then that we started selling wine and beer, and that helped us a lot.

"You Should Come Work for Us"

It had been about six months, when the big shots from Eagle Thrifty in Reno came and stopped by the store.

"Idaho, can we walk in your store?" they asked.

"Sure, you guys let me walk in your store. Come in."

Ignacio and Marceline Urrutia, 1980. Photograph by Jeff Fontana.

There were three of them, and one said, "What do you plan to do? Are you going to have a grocery store after all? You should come work for us."

"No, you guys fired me. Once I get fired, I won't go to work for the same company. I am going to stick around here, and one of these days I will have a grocery store."

"I don't know, things are pretty tough. You have to have money, you know."

Urrutia realized that the guys knew how tight his situation with the money was. They saw that he didn't have much merchandise in the store. Nevertheless, there was no chance that he would allow himself to be swayed from his lifelong dream. No chance at all. He continued building the stock little by little, drawing as little money as possible. The revenue that came in went into purchasing more merchandise.

A year later, the fellows from Eagle Thrifty came back again, and by then Idaho Grocery was looking a little better and fuller. One of them, apparently impressed, said, "I thought you said you were going to have a little store. You don't know about these Bascos, they'll do anything. I see you have a real store now; that is why we want you to come back and work for us."

"You guys didn't treat me right. If you had, I should be managing the Eagle Thrifty business in Susanville," Urrutia replied.

Eagle Thrifty had good business for a while, but three to four years later they sold out to a company from Sacramento, Raley's, which did not last either and in turn sold to Shop'n Save.

"But Idaho Grocery is still here," Urrutia says proudly, yet without pomposity.

However, in 1971 the budding enterprise suffered a serious setback. As a result of a botched operation, the butcher Michel Irribarren, who was then a partner, became gravely ill and was rushed to Reno, where a month later he died at age twenty-nine. He had recently married and left a wife and a young child. In spite of the tragedy, business was improving steadily. It took the Urrutias a little longer to build it, because they started with nothing. Urrutia always stresses the hard work that went into it. "That's what it takes," he adds with conviction.

Marceline and Ignacio Urrutia
at a wedding in Bilbao, Bizkaia,
1970.

Idaho in the Local News

By the 1980s, Urrutia's children were growing up and beginning to help out a little in the store. Idaho Grocery was fast becoming a community fixture in Susanville. People could go there and buy groceries, meats, and so much more. It was a mercantile store, in fact.

On May 16, 1980, the *Lassen Advocate* of Susanville published in its weekly section a full-page color photograph of Mr. and Mrs. Urrutia.[1] Under the heading LASSEN LAND, the couple appear in their store, smiling and holding choice fruit in their hands. The article's two full pages, entitled A TOUGH ROAD TO SUCCESS, were written by Jeff Fontana and summarized Urrutia's saga and the history of their lives in Susanville. Six photographs illustrated the story, five by Fontana and one dated 1947, showing Mr. Idaho between two large banana bundles in the Royal Grocery. The Urrutia children, Reneé and Joey, are featured in the other photographs, as well as Vernon Silva, the butcher.

The 1980s were a decisive time for the Idaho Grocery. The *Lassen Advocate* stated that "the fate of the store now hangs in limbo," indicating that it would remain open only if the four children decided to continue with it, which was not clear back then. "If they do, they will have to work as hard as I," was Urrutia's advice to his children, according to the article. "There is no other way a little guy can make it, everything costs so much," he said, referring to wages and the price of the products. "You have to work long hard hours and keep up with it." Urrutia attributed his success to the fact that he came with the experience he acquired in his family business in Galdakao. "It must be in my blood. . . . Some people might think 'oh he's just another Basque,' but I look at my life differently. I came here with nothing, and I made it."[2]

On February 6, 1996, the local paper, *Lassen County Times*, ran an article written by Joseph Kreiss featuring a biographical summary of Urrutia in the United States. MR. IDAHO's LIFE TESTAMENT TO U.S. WORK ETHIC, the title ran. Urrutia had just turned eighty-three, but the paper said that watching him work "you might think he was forty years younger."

After paraphrasing the story that had appeared in another local paper in 1980, Kreiss went on to emphasize Urrutia's Basque background and his fifty-two years in the grocery business:

> The Basque grocer is a living success story, a lesson to the younger generation about the old work ethic. "If you want to make it in life, you have to work for it,"

Idaho states as a matter of fact. Many of Idaho's critics told him that he was crazy, and that the bigger stores would put him out of business. "I had courage. I am Basque. I'll die before I surrender," he said proudly.[3]

Kreiss, as a way of highlighting the work ethic issue, touches on the long hours Urrutia put in the store:

> He gets up about 3 A.M. and is in the store an hour later, seven days a week. "You have to be here to see the people coming in. . . . That's how you make it in this business. At 10 A.M. Idaho goes home for a nap and his main meal of the day. He returns to the store by 3 P.M. until closing time at 7 P.M. Before he used to close at 10–11 P.M. It's a family business and wife Marceline and sons, Joey and Robert and daughter Reneé work in the store. "I enjoy having the family close to me," he said. "I've taught my family about work. My mother lived to be ninety-nine years old and I plan to keep on working."

Finally, Kreiss says that Urrutia's life philosophy is embodied in President John F. Kennedy's famous statement, "It is not what your country can do for you, it's what you can do for your country."[4]

TEN

Visiting the Basque Country

. . . . .

As the Urrutia children became older, they began taking on more and more of the duties at the store, which afforded Mr. and Mrs. Urrutia some leisure, even time to visit their families in Europe. Urrutia returned to the Old Country in 1957 with Marceline and Mary Jane, who still remembers how she rode the donkey up and down the hills at the farmstead in Esterenzubi, where her mother was born. Urrutia bought a Kodak movie camera for this trip and brought back rare films of the relatives and other places they visited.

In 1970 the whole Urrutia family made a trip to the Basque Country. First, they went to Bizkaia, and from Spain they went to Iparralde in France. The children became acquainted with all the *amatxis* (grandmothers) and many relatives in the Old Country.

Robert and Joey remember an episode that happened to them while vacationing in Iparralde. A few of their relative farmers were haying and, needing extra rakes and pitchforks, the two boys were sent to their barn to get some. The farm was higher up on the hill and, instead of walking down with the rakes, the boys thought they would borrow an old bike. They hopped on it, and as Joey tried to hang on and not lose the implements he was clutching, Robert was alarmed to discover that the speeding bike had no brakes. The two brothers were headed straight for a barbed-wire fence. As he told the story in 1999, Robert was still feeling the tense moments experienced many years ago. "Thank

Petra Urrutia, Ignacio's mother, Galdakao, Bizkaia, 1980.

Marceline and Ignacio Urrutia at the Idaho Grocery, next to the 4-H beef they bought at auction, Susanville, California, 1986.

God that Dad kicked the bike from under us, otherwise we would have been decapitated by the fence," he says.

Urrutia has made a total of six trips to Europe in 1950, 1957, 1970, 1982, 1986, and 1991. Of course, he always kept in touch with his mother, Petra Urrutia, and the family. For years, he sent her a big bouquet of flowers on her birthday, which was on June 15. In Galdakao, the family would gather to celebrate her birthday with a big dinner and take photographs, which were sent to California. During dinner time, Urrutia called his mother and he talked with everybody. In

1982 Urrutia missed her birthday but arrived in the Basque Country shortly afterward.

In Galdakao, Petra Urrutia continued attending to the business at the store. Whenever he went back for a visit, the owner of Idaho Grocery enjoyed comparing how identical businesses were run in California and in Bizkaia. He jotted down the main differences:

> Mother still sits by the check stand. They use the same old drawer, like I used to. You pull it out, and the money is all there, bills, change. . . . Every once in a while she gets all the big bills, and she puts them in a packet and then she goes to hide it in the bedroom. She doesn't want to keep too many [bills] in the drawer, because, who knows? Somebody might walk in and rob the place or something. The bills are one thousand, five thousand, ten thousand *pesetas,* and so forth, because the *peseta* is not worth much anymore.[1] When I first saw all the big bills, I thought, "My goodness, look at all the money." But it wasn't as much as the numbers suggested.

One day Petra Urrutia half jokingly said to him, "Son, I still like the money." She was ninety then. A lady nearby waiting in line heard her and responded, "So do we, Petra, so do we."

Petra continued working at the family store in Galdakao as long as she could, and that was a long time; when she died in 1991, she was ninety-nine years old.

Changes in the Old Country

An emigrant is perhaps the best appraiser of the changes that through the decades may occur in a given country. In 1931 Urrutia left a Basque Country that was still largely rural, except for the Bilbao area, Eibar, and a few other cities, which were industrialized or undergoing fast and heavy industrialization. Since his departure, Urrutia has observed profound changes. He noticed, for example, that food prices seemed pretty high, but that "people are making good money—maybe because they have good unions—and they live better than we do," he remarked.

Prosperity has arrived since the late 1950s, because when I went back nineteen years later it was the same. No change. Those were the years under the Franco dictatorship. The streetcars were dirty, with all the paint chipped off. They were the same ones as I remembered. I rode some of them, and they looked like they were about to go off the tracks. This one conductor was driving wildly, and I said to him, "What do you think you are carrying in here? Stock animals?" That was in 1950. All these ladies standing in there were trying to hang onto the ropes. I thought it was kind of dangerous. The driver took the curves so fast that I said to him, "Can't you slow down?" He gave me a dirty look; he didn't like it. He probably knew I was a foreigner, the way I talked. A lady defended the driver and told me to mind my own business. And I said, "I will talk. I come from a country where you can say what you think is right."

When he arrived in the train station in Bilbao, after he had left Madrid, as soon as he stepped off the train he was confronted with a curious situation: two suitcase handlers competing with each other for the privilege of carrying his luggage. They were two light pieces, and Urrutia thought it ridiculous to have someone else carry them, but on hindsight, the whole thing was a simple affair: the men were trying to make a living and wanted a tip. Those were hard times in the 1950s.

In 1957, when Urrutia returned home, he already saw some changes, which accelerated in the 1960s. Factories were producing and exporting, and the economy was on the upswing. He could hardly believe the new situation. Of course, they had some economic problems the same way as they had them in the United States. Life in the Basque Country continued improving. He noticed more freedom and fewer worries. Televisions and cars were everywhere, and the bars were always full of people.

After work, people stopped for a *txikito* (small drink of wine) at different bars, where they discussed soccer and other sports or which one was the next game to be shown on TV, etc. Often it would be two hours before they went home for supper. Every day was like that. They were enjoying life, all right. His old buddies in Galdakao wanted him to tag along from bar to bar drinking *txikitos*, but Urrutia could not keep up with them. "You boys go ahead. I am not used to this kind of life," he had to tell them.

"Boy, some of them guys drank ten to twelve *txikitos*.[2] After eating supper, a few still returned to the local bar to play cards with their friends." The preferred card game was *mus* (pronounced "moose").[3]

Even as a boy growing up in Galdakao, Urrutia was never fond of bars, poolhalls, smoking, and drinking, which were the favorite pastimes of his Basque friends in Idaho, too.[4] He didn't understand the *mus* game, though he played it a couple of times when his friends were one person short. He preferred being outside breathing fresh air. "When I was young, we had fewer bars in the Old Country," he says. But of course, during his youth Galdakao had a population of seven thousand and now it is over fifty thousand, which is mostly due to Spanish immigration.

Another great revolution he observed was the roads, the cars, and the freeways. Today when leaving Bilbao by car you take the freeway and you can miss Galdakao very easily, because the freeway goes around it. Nothing like taking the old highway with horse and wagon in Urrutia's days.

There is traffic, boy! I stay outside on the sidewalk and the cars never stop, and if I go farther down to the freeway, the cars are traveling at a hundred miles per hour. You cannot even get on the highway, there is that much traffic.

When Urrutia goes for a visit, he enjoys walking in the same old nooks and crannies that he used to in his younger days. The old factory where explosives were manufactured is still there. "They have a different system now, completely advanced and safe." In the old days, they had less safety, and people sometimes died in accidents. Now it is all quiet, and you don't hear any such things.

Urrutia also went to Bekelarri, where he spent the first six years of his life. In 1950 he saw trenches dug by Basque soldiers during the Spanish Civil War of 1936–1939. The Basques were trying to resist the German air force that functioned at the service of Spanish General Franco, but the airplanes had machines guns, and many Basque soldiers were killed right in the trenches. The Lekue-Sagarminagas left the farmstead for fear of the Germans and Italians,[5] Urrutia says, and his grandmother died apparently in an accident while she was on a train to France.

While most farmsteads in the Basque Country were modernized in the 1970s and 1980s, with indoor plumbing and all the conveniences found in town, Urrutia found that the Bekelarri farmstead "still looked pretty old because there had been no repairs made." So to this day, Bekelarri retains a measure of "old world" cultural flavor that Urrutia knew as a small boy. He thinks that it is possible that the Lekue-Sagarminaga children moved to town and visit the old farmstead only occasionally.

Changes in the Church

The old Church of Andra Mari[6] where Urrutia learned to play handball is still there, seemingly impervious to time, though it has undergone some repairs. Inside, they changed the altars in order to accommodate modern liturgy, but for the most part it looks the same. People do not attend church like in the old days. Older women and men, especially, go to funerals and to the many masses that are said for the deceased throughout the year. For example, a lot of masses for Petra Urrutia have been ordered, and the family and friends attend such services religiously.

One big change in the church relates to the clergy, or the absence of priests. There used to be five priests serving Galdakao in Urrutia's time, but now there is only one. Old memories stream to Urrutia's mind:

> Don Prudencio used to live by the church—in the rectory—he was a big priest. He spent time sitting on his balcony. I passed by with my horse and wagon, and I looked up and there he was, Don Prudencio praying and looking up to the skies. See, those days they had their devotions, the priests did. They prayed by the crucifix, doing penance, and such things. They threw a kiss on the air, to God, I guess. Every day I passed by, and Don Prudencio didn't even know I went through. He just kept praying.

During his visit to Bizkaia in 1982, Urrutia ran into the resident priest, who was about thirty-two to thirty-four years old. Urrutia walked a lot during his vacation, and one day, as he strolled by, he saw the priest sitting by the church and reading a book. This is how Urrutia remembers their encounter:

> I stopped and said in Spanish, "Hello, Father." He was talking to me in Spanish—well, started in Spanish—and I did, too. Pretty soon, I said, "*Euskalduna?*" and he answered: "*Ni bai, euskaldun jaioa*" (I am, I am a born Basque speaker). But he wanted to go back to the Spanish language, I don't know why. So, he started

to ask me questions about the United States. About the religion, how the Catholics act, and all the religions we have . . .I told him how many churches we had in Susanville.

"We have one Catholic priest in our church," I said.

"Well, the same here," he replied.

"Fifty-one years ago, there were five priests [in Galdakao]."

"You've been gone fifty-one years?"

"Yes. I used to live in that house down there. Used to be a store in that corner."

"That's a long time ago. I wasn't here then."

The priest seemed to be surprised and asked again where Urrutia used to live and other such details.

"I left when King Alfonso left," Urrutia said.

"Did you have something to do with politics?"

"No. He left, and it was my time to leave, too, because I had my plans. The king left on April 14, 1931, and I left on the 21st. He went to France, and I went to England."

"That's a coincidence. Is your family here?"

"Yes, my family lives in that house," Urrutia said, pointing.

"Oh, that's your mother? She didn't come to church today."

"She would have if she had somebody to give her a ride, but she won't walk up the hill."

Urrutia explained that the last time he went to the Basque Country, he had a car and he used to bring his mother to church every day, but this time he did not buy or rent one. Driving around Susanville is no problem, but in Galdakao the traffic is much worse and everybody drives fast. He wanted to relax and be free of the hassles of driving. That way, he spent more time with his mother.

One of Petra Urrutia's daily routines was listening to mass on the radio, which lasted about half an hour. For her, it was the same as being in church. She said to her son, "Do you want to come in and listen to the mass?" and he responded, "Sure," and he sat right next to her. She pulled out her rosary and she prayed. "That's what I call religion," Urrutia says. His half-sisters, too, went to church every day, before they opened the store, which is a five-minute walk away. "They are younger than me, so they are faster. They walk fast in the Old Country. They never go slow," he says.

Basque Politics

Urrutia summarizes his views on the matter of the political situation in his homeland from the 1930s through the 1980s:

> When they overthrew the king, the country was in bad shape. They wanted a change, a different way to live, but I don't think they gained anything. During the many trips that I made back to the Old Country, Franco was in power [1939–1975]. I never said a word, never spoke up. Different people had different political views, but I said nothing while I was there. I did not like Franco, because he killed all my friends that I went to school with. Nice kids. If I had been there, I would have been in the bullets, too, yeah, because we were *Bizkaitarrak* [pro-independence Basques]. It should be a free country. Can't you have your own ideas and have a say on how you will live and your way? Well, over there, they won't let you. Franco wanted to get rid of all Basqueness, erase all of it. I say, that's wrong. One time, after I made my first trip, I was walking around the Church of Andra Mari, and I saw the names of the people who had

been killed right there. And I said to my friends, "Well, that's so and so. I went to school with him." And they said, "Yes, they were killed right here as they walked in front of the church." I think that's wrong.

I don't have to live there in that situation, but now [in the post-Franco era] I think people have their vengeance, that's what's going on now, a counteraction against the past thirty-five years. These kids suffered when they were little, they endured the death of their folks, so now is payback time. Any country will do that, I don't care if it is Beirut or Jerusalem. Those kids saw their fathers killed in the street, and they cannot forget it. Of course they cannot get even with the same people who killed their folks, but with their generation. Your folks killed mine, now is my turn. They gain nothing on it.[7]

ELEVEN

The Good Life in Susanville

· · · · ·

The last two decades of the century were generally good years for the Urrutia family. The children were grown and married, and Ignacio and Marceline were happy together. They have nine grandchildren. The Urrutias are members of the Catholic Church and the Susanville Basque Club, which in 1993 nominated Marceline as Mother of the Year.

The Urrutias preserve fond memories of their years in Susanville. They enjoy an enviable reputation in town, and every day they meet a lot of friendly faces. In fact, more than once Mr. Idaho was encouraged to run for mayor of Susanville, to which he responds, "If I did, I would make too many changes, and I don't think they would like it."

This writer asked him to share a particular incident he might remember, and this is what he told me in Basque:

> It was 1971, I think, and even though we didn't take too many vacations and we didn't gamble, this one time Marceline and I went to John Ascuaga's Nugget in Sparks, Nevada, to watch a show. On the floor we met Frank Arostegui from Idaho, Cruza Arostegui's son, whom we knew. He was a pit boss. We had dinner and went to the show, and as we were leaving the show-room we were approached by a waitress. She was carrying a platter on which we were handed $37 in cash with a note COMPLIMENTS OF JOHN ASCUAGA. We had not even seen John, but he was returning the money

we had spent. In the end, we spent the money anyway, not in gambling, but on food. I don't believe in gambling.

Basque entrepreneurs in the West are good at patronizing each other's businesses. Whenever Urrutia traveled to Idaho, for example, he stopped at the Winnemucca Hotel in Winnemucca, Nevada, which the Mike Olano family has owned for some twenty-five years. In fact, one day in May 1999, Urrutia looked in his drawer and came up with Olano's business card. On the back there was a personal greeting for Urrutia, written by Olano in Basque and Spanish. It was not dated, but it seemed over twenty years old.

More Than Just a Business

The business part sometimes conflicted with family life, but it was seldom allowed to overshadow it. The store was like another home, which kept the family together and close. The Urrutia residence, being just two blocks away, was also very convenient, for example, for baby-sitting the grandchildren.

As noted, the children began helping out in the store when they became teenagers. By the time Mary Jane turned fifteen, she was assisting at the cash register. In addition, she did some bookkeeping, she wrote checks, made bank deposits, etc.[1] As Reneé recalls:

> My sister Mary Jane, the oldest, started helping Dad clean up the store and doing chores like that. I started at thirteen, but when Robert came in, since he was the youngest, he would tell Mom, "I cannot be working, I am just a kid." But he was a wonderful worker, very clean, and my dad was very pleased. Robert was thirteen to fourteen by then. Joey, the older brother, had been helping out for several years already.

As Mr. Idaho would say, his children learned that work does not kill. They inherited valuable work ethics from him.

Robert remembers that they used to get a $30 weekly allowance, which was quite a bit of money, but it went into their savings account. It was hard work, but Dad would say, "This is a vacation. Working in the logging camp and in the sheep . . . now, that was hard work."

Joey says, "During the Depression, Dad was making ten cents an hour. Now, that's pressure." Robert points at a large white metal container outside and remarks, "See that cooler? Dad would go get groceries with his pickup truck, store them in there, and peddle them house-to-house." Joey adds, "We learned a lot from Dad. We don't know what an eight-hour day or a five-day week is."

Soon after Reneé returned to work after Doyle's birth, she brought him to the store in a bassinet and people loved it. When he became about three months old, he was harder to handle and *Ama* (mother) kept him until 5 P.M., at which time Reneé picked him up, and Marceline would join her husband in the store until closing time at 7 P.M.

Reneé also remembers when she, Joey, and Robert were little, and it was their sister, Mary Jane, who was older, who put them to bed. Then, about 11 P.M., Reneé woke up to the smell of food being cooked. For her, that was a sure sign that "Mom and Dad are home." But when everyone was at the store, that, too, felt like a second home. Reneé says:

> Our lives revolved around our parents and their lives
> revolved around us. They helped us raise our children.
> Our children are very lucky to have known and en-
> joyed their grandparents. We didn't have that. Those
> were wonderful years with our parents and our families
> together. We would get together on holidays and birth-
> days with good food and fun.

Throughout the years, the Urrutias hired a number of people at their store, and they, too, were treated like family. Verda Chittock, for example, worked many years for them, and she was very close to Marceline. In fact, they called each other sisters.

Every Fourth of July, the Urrutias had a big barbecue for the family, friends, workers, and associates. Marceline cooked for everybody, and everyone had a grand time. After the barbecue in the evening, the grandkids enjoyed their fireworks, and afterward everybody settled down and sat outside to watch the fireworks being displayed at the fairgrounds. "We all had perfect seats," observes Reneé.

The Grocery Business: 1980s–1990s

In 1999 Idaho Grocery is still in business and doing well. Asked to assess his past years in the trade, these are some of Urrutia's thoughts:

> In 1975 I bought the building from the owner. In 1982 it was paid for in full. My hard work proved itself. That was my policy all my life, work and work. Play, no, I didn't have that intention. I worked hard in the Old Country, and from the hardness of the Old Country I learned that in this country you have to work to make a living just the same as in the Old Country. But in the United States, with more freedom, you can accomplish more of the things which you want to do. When I left the Old Country, there was no money to start a business, no opportunity either, because people did not give you a chance like in this country.

Speaking with Urrutia in 1999, this was his assessment of current business in the town of Susanville:

> Our competition is great, but we still can compete because we have good merchandise: good meat and good produce. Today the store is thriving. We have more stores than ever in town, that is more competition. But we have steady customers. We have USDA choice beef. We offer

butcher services to the local ranchers and game hunters: we cut the meat, custom wrap it, and store it in the freezer. Typical beef is about six hundred pounds, and we charge forty cents per pound, and the packages are stamped NOT FOR SALE. My son Joey goes to the ranches and kills the beef, pork, and lamb. He has a truck equipped with a winch and he brings the carcass to the store. We hang it for fourteen days before cutting it. Robert and others cut the meat.

In 1989 we refurbished the store building with new siding and other improvements. Above the store, there are four apartments, and a beauty shop used to be in the rear. The business part has five cold storages: one cooler for beef, one for fruit and produce, one for beer and soft drinks, and two freezers for meats.

The Urrutia philosophy is that the little guy must always look out for ways to earn or save a penny. That is why in 1984 the family embarked into a side business: cardboard compacting. The story was told on May 23, 1999, as Mr. Idaho, Reneé, and Robert were sitting at the table and enjoying a delicious late Sunday lunch cooked by Reneé. Joey was on duty at the store and joined the gathering later. Large stores in town all had their cardboard compactors, but none of the little ones did. Idaho Grocery was producing a lot of trash, which was picked up three times a week, and year in, year out, at $130 per pick-up per month, it was a considerable cash drain. In 1984 they decided to invest $12,000 on a brand-new cardboard compactor. Robert confessed that he was uneasy about the soundness of the idea, but Urrutia quickly adds that the machine paid for itself in no time. Robert laughs and says, "My father is happy as long as he is making a penny, but I rather think in terms of dollars, not pennies."

When the machine arrived, Urrutia went to businesses around town, loading up all the cardboard boxes on his pickup. Suddenly, in the back of the store they had stacks of cardboard bundles, each worth $20 then. Pretty soon, the fire department sent them a complaint notice stating that the cardboard posed a fire hazard for the offices of Lassen National Forest Service, which were housed in the adjacent building. "They were worried about the Forest Service offices. They weren't worried about our store burning down," Urrutia says jokingly.

Actually, the cardboard compactor was more than just a money matter. Ecologically, it made a lot of sense to recycle, and by eliminating some of the trash, the businesses in town were saving on garbage charges as well. It was a win-win situation for everybody. Robert says that it took a lot of man-hours to feed the compactor. Today, they get $8 per cardboard load, not much perhaps, but the bottom line is not what you make but how much you save. Without the machine, the garbage pick-up bill would be $390 a month.

They still have the compactor machine, but Robert says, "We don't pick up cardboard anymore."

"We don't have time. Well, we have time but we don't go. It's paid for," adds Mr. Urrutia.

His remark sounded a bit sarcastic and everybody had a big laugh. He continued, "I wish I was young again. I'd make millions. In the old days, I drove around town looking at people's lawns, and if the grass was a bit high I went to the door and offered to cut it for a dollar. A dollar was a dollar back then."

Butchering and Meat Cutting

Idaho Grocery began selling meat in the early years, but when Michel Iribarren died in 1971, Urrutia had to hire a butcher. It turned out that, through the years, the meat department was actually losing money. Robert discovered that some of the meat was wasted, causing a $1,500–$2,000 drain in the business every month. The "leak" was plugged when Joey and

Marceline and Ignacio Urrutia gather in the company of their grandchildren to celebrate Ignacio's birthday, Susanville, California, January 31, 1996. Left to right: Jessie, Casey, Jolea, Ignacio, Triston, Luke, Kendall, Marceline, and Doyle.

Robert took over the meat department, and business has been thriving ever since. Of great help was the advice that local butchers and meat cutters like Jerry Quam and Norman Palmer provided when the Urrutia brothers were learning the meat business.

The year 1986 was particularly important, for that is when they started custom slaughtering. They financed the purchase of a 1986 Ford F-350, and they outfitted it with a stainless steel box, winch, back lights, power outlets, and other essentials required for butchering farm animals on the spot. Joey remembers that when they bought the truck, the bookkeeper told them that they were spending their father's retirement.

Three months later, when the truck was finally delivered, the two brothers were ready. "We were hungry for business," Robert recalls. Just then, another mobile butchering service in Johnstonville—their competitor—offered to sell Idaho his truck for half the price. They bought it, and now Joey and Robert each were going to ranches and butchering animals, which they brought to the store for cutting and wrapping.

As it turned out, they were butchering so much that they had a difficult time cutting the meat. Therefore, they decided that Joey would run the butchering truck, and Robert would stay in the store and break the carcasses. Joey enjoys his work, which is rather seasonal. He kills between three hundred and four hundred animals a year. He covers the Susanville area but also Sierra Valley and occasionally goes to Alturas, Northern Nevada, and even California's Central Valley. Behind the truck he pulls a small trailer with fifty-five gallon drums to store the offal, which he takes to the dump.

Many ranchers eat the beef they raise, and that is what offering them butchering services is all about.[2] Obviously, Idaho Grocery does not sell the beef that Joey brings from the ranches, but one time the state inspector showed up in Susanville and questioned Joey about it.

As Joey describes the incident, it was one time in February when business was slow, and Joey had gone to Nevada to butcher a couple of hogs. As he came across the fruit inspection station at the California border, the guard asked him about the hogs in the truck and wrote a report about it, which eventually arrived in Sacramento in the office of the state meat inspection. They sent an inspector to Susanville to find out what the boys at Idaho Grocery were up to, as Joey puts it. When the man started asking questions, Joey simply told him, "We don't do that [sell the beef], never have." The inspector replied, "Good answer," and he left town satisfied.

Written with red letters on the white metal box on the back of the truck is the only advertisement of the Urrutia business. Joey says it's enough. "I travel all over this valley with my truck, and a lot of people see the Idaho Grocery name."

The meat department (butchering included) today is a

much more important part of Idaho Grocery than it ever was, comprising up to 50 percent of the whole operation. Business has doubled since 1986. "We are the only ones in town who sell USDA choice meat," says Robert. Reneé adds:

> People come to us for quality beef. They will come up and say, "We are having a nice dinner." That means they want some quality cuts, which they trust we can provide. They might even ask for cooking suggestions, which we are happy to offer.

Changing and Diversifying

In the old days, Idaho Grocery was a mercantile store and sold just about everything besides groceries: brooms, charcoal, hardware, tools, auto parts, and toys. But things changed, and it was converted into a convenience store.

"We wouldn't be in business today if we were a regular grocery store," Robert states.

In the late 1980s, the city of Susanville undertook the major task of overhauling the main street, which was closed for almost a year. The businesses were severely affected by the closure, and the Urrutia family began looking for other sources of income, such as wholesaling. It began modestly at first, working with a few local restaurants, but it has grown to about 40 percent of the business.

Today Reneé, Joey, and Robert carry the brunt of the business load. Until July 1999 Mr. Idaho was never far away. His favorite task was babying the produce by covering it with several layers of wet fabric before closing the shop, all the while complaining that no one cared about produce anymore. That does not mean that he does not take it easy. Just checking on nature's progress in his large and elaborate yard would take several hours. He has a garden where leeks are growing and surely tomatoes will be planted soon in its rich earth. Urrutia, like so many other Basques in the West,

The Urrutia extended family at the St. Francis Hotel on the occasion of Ignacio being honored with the Distinguished Service Award, Susanville, California, November 8, 1996. Left to right: Robert Urrutia with his wife, Michelle, Kay (Joey's wife), Marceline, Joey, Ignacio (holding the award), Reneé and her husband, Ronnie Jones, and granddaughter Danielle, with Scott Rivers.

has nearly a dozen fruit trees arranged around the yard, among them plums, apples, and cherries, and also grapevines. A variety of shade trees are planted on the outer perimeter, which is also lined with flowers galore.

Sitting in an easy chair in his lush backyard, one can contemplate the splendor of the snowy mountains in the Lassen National Forest. For a man like Urrutia it is the perfect setting to reflect on his adventurous, fortunate, and prosperous long life.

Looking back, the family realizes that it took a lot of hard work to make the business into the successful venture that it is today. Now, Reneé, Joey, and Robert have children of their own, and they are perhaps looking forward to shorter days at the store.

Mr. Idaho Honored

Mr. Idaho, as most people call him, probably knows more people in Susanville than any other individual in town. For more than half a century, he has seen most everyone come to the stores where he worked. It was in this spirit of dedication and stability that on November 8, 1996, the Lassen County Farm Bureau honored Urrutia with the Distinguished Service Award. The annual dinner ceremony was held at the St. Francis Hotel in Susanville, where the local Farm Bureau recognized Urrutia as the fourth member of the community to be deserving of the award. A few days later, the local paper carried the news in a feature article by Joseph Kreiss that commended Urrutia for being "our kind of guy."[3]

The following includes excerpts from the statement by incoming Farm Bureau president Hannah Tangeman Cheney during the award ceremony:

> Lassen County Farm Bureau is honoring an individual, a business, and a family that embodies the small business

The Urrutia family. Left to right: Robert, Reneé, Ignacio, Mary Jane, and Joey, June 1999.

and generational ethic that is so much a part of agriculture. . . . [Urrutia] is very much a success story in his family and his business. He works farmer's hours and his business savvy and ability to satisfy the needs of his loyal customers has kept him in business at a time when small is very rare.[4]

Furthermore, Urrutia was praised for his support of youth activities in Susanville and as an example for all the community. Receiving the award, Urrutia thanked the Farm Bureau and vowed to never forget it. And once again, he took the occasion to plug one of his favorite slogans, "Don't ever give up. Keep working. This is a country like no other country. God bless America."

In an interview in May 1999, Urrutia and his son Robert spoke of community involvement and helping the less fortunate in Susanville. Urrutia also spoke of people taking advantage of credit or writing bad checks for merchandise they purchased at their store. "*Hainbat jende mantendu dut nik hemen*"[5] (I have fed a great many people from this place), he said, referring to food that was never paid for. For example, one time someone wrote a check for $500, which turned out to be no good.

In March 1999, once again Susanville recognized Mr. Idaho's contributions to the community when he was nominated for the "Favorite Older Worker Award" for 1999. The acknowledgment was sponsored by the Lassen Career Network, and although he did not receive the top prize, he was recognized as the oldest of the nominees.

"Gone Fishing"

Ever since Idaho Grocery opened in 1968, one of the things that customers came to depend on was its being open. For years, Idaho opened the store by 5 A.M. and would not close it until 10 or 11 P.M. Every day. You could almost call it an early version of a convenience store. "We never closed," Urrutia says flatly, but of course there were a few exceptions—for example, when Reneé and Robert got married. Joey's wedding was later in the evening, and they didn't have to close.

On certain holidays when all other stores were closed, Urrutia remained open for those who needed to shop. He remembers that, in fact, there were quite a few shoppers. "The people looked like Indians circling the wagons," he says, borrowing a line from western movies, no doubt.

There was one day when Idaho Grocery broke all the rules and closed. It was the summer of 1991, and they put up a big sign on the door that said WE HAVE GONE FISHING. The occasion was a visit by relatives from Narrosse, France. Jean Louis Chirumbero and his wife, Jeanine, with their two sons, Jean and François, came to visit them and stayed in Susanville for a while.

The Urrutias decided to take a day off and show their relatives a good time. They borrowed a boat from a friend, and they all went to Lake Almanor, where they swam, water skied, and had a picnic. Everyone had a wonderful time, especially the boys from the Old Country, where they do not have lakes like they do in the United States. They have the ocean, but the lake was something new for them. From Susanville, the Chirumbero family proceeded to Miles City, Montana, to see other relatives.

At the time, Ignacio Urrutia was in Bizkaia on account of his mother's death. Reneé said, "We were sure that Dad would hear about the 'gone fishing' sign when he returned, which he did."

Through the years, other relatives also came to Susanville. *Tanta* (aunt) Gracianne Chirumbero and her family arrived in 1984 and stayed for a long visit. Manolita and Jose

Doistua, *tío* (uncle) Manuel Diego and *tía* (aunt) Concha from Mexico, *tío* Jesus Diego from Spain, and niece Maria Jose Doistua from Bilbao.

Marceline Urrutia's Death: 1998

The Urrutias were partners in the grocery store business. Once the children were raised and attending school, Marceline joined her husband and worked long hours at the Idaho Grocery side-by-side with her husband. Like her husband, she always greeted their customers with a smile. Reneé says:

> Mom was a big part of the business. People were used to seeing her at the store all the time. People came to the store for more than just groceries, because Marceline was a listener. "She was the reason for half of the business."

Besides being the best *ama* (mother) and *amatxi* (grand-mother), Marceline, like many Basque women, was a wonderful cook and prepared many Old Country dishes. "We liked everything she cooked," her children agreed in chorus.

Robert told of an 1978 incident that reveals how proud Marceline was of her culinary skills. Robert was the hunter in the family, and one day he brought home a Canada goose that he had killed. The big bird kept Marceline busy for most of the day, plucking it first—with Robert's help—and then cooking it. When the bird was finally brought to the dinner table, it was found to be palatable, but dry. "Oh, shoot," Marceline said, disappointed. That was her only failure with fowl. Her other game birds, like pheasants and chukars, cooked in wine, always turned out delicious.

Marceline died rather unexpectedly in 1998. She had recently remodeled her kitchen, and six months earlier Idaho Grocery had been made into a legal corporation, so that she and Idaho could take more time off and travel. But it was not going to be. This was a difficult year for the Urrutia family. In March and April, Idaho was off work with bursitis and aching joints, which severely limited his mobility, though it didn't keep him too many days away from being at the store during closing time. People were aware that Idaho was ill, and that is why they were even more shocked when suddenly they heard of Marceline's passing away.

In early June, Marceline went to San Francisco for her granddaughter's graduation. The week before, she had gone to the doctor for a physical checkup, and when she returned she announced to the family that everything was fine, "blood pressure OK, too," she said, according to Reneé. In San Francisco she felt fine, though a bit tired, and in the evenings when she called her husband, she complained about the cool and damp weather in the Bay Area. She was used to the dry Susanville climate.

When she returned from the Bay Area for the First Communion of the grandchildren, she looked fine, but a few days later, when Idaho and Marceline went out for a walk after dinner, suddenly she ran out of breath, and they had to get back to the house right away. Yet that same night, Idaho remembers, at bedtime, she grabbed him with both hands and raised him off his chair without any apparent difficulty. "She always said whenever she did not feel well. This time she did not say anything," recalls Idaho.

Apparently Marceline didn't know that her death was near, and she worried about her husband's bursitis. The day before she died, Reneé went over to pick up her son, Doyle, whom Marceline was baby-sitting, and found her father struggling to get up from the table. Marceline looked at him and said to her daughter, "Reneé, *aita ez da ontsa, ez da ontsa*" (Reneé, Father is not well, not well at all).

In the early hours of June 24, 1998, Marceline had a heart attack and died in the morning of the next day.[6] When Idaho noticed something amiss, he called Reneé, and the following was the short exchange that took place between them:

"Reneé, Mom won't wake up."

"Is she breathing?"

"Of course, she is snoring."

Immediately, several 911 calls were made, and Reneé jumped into her car to drive over to her parents' place. "My sister-in-law Michelle came [to the house] first, and she did CPR on her," Reneé says. Marceline was taken by ambulance to the local hospital and put on life support. Reneé called the Catholic priest who, as soon as he finished saying the 8 A.M. mass, went to the hospital to administer the last rites and anoint her with the sacred oil. Then Marceline was flown to Reno to determine if she was brain dead. She was in Reno about twenty-four hours, and she died at about 7:30 A.M.

The family was not ready to lose their *ama* and *amatxi* so suddenly, to say the least. A black wreath was placed on the door of the store, and when the customers came they found it closed and wondered why. Soon the sad news was known and spread quickly in town. Reneé, still struggling with the painful memories, summarizes the events of those days:

> Many came to pay their respects. Many shrubs, plants, and flowers were delivered. Cards came in the mail by the bundles. The church was full of family friends and store patrons. The Susanville Catholic priest, Father Robert Brooks, and Father Martxel Tillous, the Basque priest from San Francisco, gave a beautiful Christian burial mass. Scripture was read by Michelle Urrutia, Laura Tew, and Cal Godman.

A love poem to *ama* entitled "A Mother's Love" was read by Mary Jane, Reneé, Joey, and Robert.

After the church services, a procession conducted by the Susanville police department was led down the main street

The Urrutia clan at the wedding of Ignacio's granddaughter, Danielle, to Scott Rivers, June 1999.

to the cemetery. The Urrutia family was deeply moved and thankful to them for their respect for Marceline and the family. Afterward, luncheon was served to all by the caring and sharing ladies at the Sacred Heart Church.

Urrutia on the United States

Several times throughout this narrative, Urrutia made the point that he never looked back, but always forward. That was the philosophy by which he lived. Urrutia's faith in the United States is unfailing. "America is a nice country. This is God's country, but people born here [Americans] don't know it. Unless you have been to other countries, you don't know how good this is." That does not mean everything is peachy or squeaky clean. For example, he says, in the old days "if you didn't give the driver's license examiner four-five bottles of whiskey, you don't pass." He took the exam three times and he failed. Yet, he says, "I have seen blind people getting [driving] licenses."

Lately he observes a trend that he does not like. As good as the economy has been under the Clinton Administration, Urrutia sees it differently because of people's spending habits:

> This is a calamity. This country is going bad. In the old days, people saved more. Now they are in the hole. They make $4,000–$5,000 a month, and they buy a house, a new truck, and a boat, but they cannot afford to pay for everything. They borrow more than they make. In one pocket, they carry the ATM and the credit cards and in the other the checkbook, and there is no money in no place. I don't have a charge machine in the store. The other day, this guy came in wanting to buy a pack of cigarettes with a credit card. When I told him I didn't take cards, he took off upset. They say you don't have to work so hard now. You got credit. Stores now advertise million-dollar giveaways, and people think they are going to get it just about any day. You go to Reno, and the casinos give you money and free drinks. What more do you want from America? Never had it like this in my time.

In other words, Urrutia is saying, is this a great country or what!

But he has reservations, because, as he figures it, how good can anything be if it is so easy to get it? Nothing precious comes without an effort. That's the Old Country philosophy that he practiced all his life and still believes in.

Life Is a Journey and a Lesson

Through years of listening to many of Urrutia's fascinating true-life adventures, his children became convinced that his story should be told. This book is the result of that seminal idea that was planted around 1980. As Joey puts it, "Many people my age talk about their parents and grandparents, but they are gone. They wished they had done something like what we are doing."

The farmstead culture of Bizkaia during the 1910s was orally transmitted through the ancient language of the Basques, Euskara, and this writer thinks that Mr. Idaho Urrutia must have heard a lot of stories in Bekelarri. It was there that he learned to tell stories and acquired the skill to capture his audience. This has been his story.

Urrutia's life is the classic success story of the poor immigrant. Historians prefer to write about successful people rather than ordinary folks, even though one is as much history as the other. Urrutia's biography, however, possesses that uncanny characteristic of an unassuming, gentle man who believed in his dreams and achieved his goal through perseverance. In the process, he made a good living for himself and his family.

I don't know if we can call Urrutia a normal man, however. His son Joey remembers the time when they went to Boise to attend a funeral, and as they approached the crowd on the stairs at the church entrance, many turned to greet them. They asked, "Is that you, Idaho?" Joey observed that people's faces lit up when they saw him. A woman standing nearby said, "Any place your dad would go, any town, he would be the mayor. He is the type of person that would accomplish whatever he had on his mind."

When in 1996 the Lassen County Farm Bureau recognized Urrutia's contributions to the community, his highlighted virtues were work ethics and service. The local paper called Urrutia "our kind of guy." That was a significant statement, meaning that in the United States one does not have to belong to a certain racial or cultural group to be considered an exemplary citizen. You don't even have to speak English without an accent or attend a certain church. That's true immigrant spirit.

Determination is an Urrutia trademark. All his life he remained a focused man. He knew what he wanted and where he wanted to go. There was never any doubt of that. He came to the United States with the idea of starting a business, preferably in sales, and though it took him thirty-five years and a lot of hard work, he finally accomplished his goal.

The reader will notice that in the process of pursuing his ambitions he was forced to overcome many hurdles. Sometimes he suffered setbacks, disappointments, even discrimination. It is interesting that the United States proclaims itself to be a country of immigrants, and rightly so. In fact, it is precisely that immigrant spirit that is largely responsible for making the United States the leading country in the world. No doubt about it. Yet, in stark contradiction to that spirit, not everyone, Urrutia included, was welcomed. The country in fact passed laws in order to keep certain groups of people out. That makes no sense in the United States.

Similarly, in this capitalistic country where money is a type of religion, people like Urrutia who wanted to make money had to travel a long and difficult road before finally he was allowed a shot at the dream. That dream provided him with fuel.

Having said that, this writer had to ask Mr. Idaho Urrutia the inevitable question, "If you could relive your life, would you do it all over again?"

The answer came easily, yet convincingly. "Yes, if I knew it would turn out this way. Life was kind of an adventure for me. My story happened the way it should."

AFTERWORD

Ignacio "Idaho" Urrutia and his whole family were very much looking forward to seeing this biography in print. One day, as we were grappling with several of the many details that most manuscripts must go through before it can be turned over to the printer, Urrutia was listening from his sickbed and with a somewhat resigned look he said to me, "*Liburu hau ez da inoiz finituko*" (This book will never be finished). I reassured him that it was practically finished. Indeed, by then he himself had read and approved every part of it. Urrutia was ill, and perhaps what he meant was that he would not see the book printed, and in the end that is what happened.

Urrutia died at home on September 11, 1999, surrounded by family. When he was diagnosed with terminal cancer, he continued leading a normal life. "I feel good," he would say as he busied himself in the store, making sure that among other things his "babies"—the vegetables—were properly "put to bed" every night. He was confined to bed for only one month, all of which he spent at home, cared for by his solicitous daughters, Mary Jane and Reneé, while his sons, Joey and Robert, kept the business running. There was no better way to end one's adventure in life.

NOTES

Introduction

1. Ignacio is Spanish for Ignatius, which is a name of Basque origin. Today, it is written *Inaki* or *Eneko,* but when Urrutia was born, only the Spanish version was allowed. The Basques, however, called him Inixio (E-nee-shee-oh), and Urrutia sounds like "Oo-rroo-tee-ah."

2. This writer was born and raised in Bizkaia in the same farming environment as Mr. Urrutia, therefore, a great deal of material presented here is familiar to me.

One. Growing Up in the Basque Mountains

1. During this time period, young Basque men from the rural areas of Bizkaia preferred to emigrate to the United States as sheepherders rather than work in factories in Bilbao.

2. Throughout the interview, Urrutia used the form *Galdakano,* which is the official form he grew up with. In normal daily speech, Basque people say "Galdako,"—just like they say "Bilbo"—for Galdakao, the written version that is used here.

3. The word is derived from Spanish. In other parts of the Basque Country, they are called *arbi.*

4. In other parts of the Basque Country, they say *txistor.*

5. Means "wide river."

Two. The New Family in Town

1. Cantabria is the region adjacent to western Bizkaia.

2. Somewhat contradicting what one reads in many publications stating that since the nineteenth century and even earlier the people around Bilbao did not speak Basque, Urrutia says that "there were Basque-speaking people everywhere you went," even in Bilbao itself.

3. Gipuzkoa had the highest percentage of Euskaldun people. Farmers in most valleys of northern Nafarroa, Behenafarroa, Zuberoa, and parts of Lapurdi were also Basque speakers. Araba had the least Euskaldun population.

4. In later decades, some female teachers taught boys, but not vice versa.

5. Other teachers had different methods, like hitting the pupils with a stick on the tip of their fingers, which was a very painful experience. By the way, during this time, corporal punishment was a universally adopted method of discipline in the western world, including the United States.

6. Urrutia says that, initially, Diego came to Bizkaia to sell *cuévanos*, which are baskets made with willows.

7. In the Basque Country and in Spain in general, women keep their last names even after marriage.

8. He means kidnapping by the *gaueko* or other witches, not by other people.

9. Elderly people and others have them delivered for a small fee.

10. Urrutia has learned this term from northern Basques in the United States. In his native Bizkaia, they say *abarketak*.

11. But there were also benches, mostly for the males.

12. The Jesuits have their university in Deusto.

Three. Life At Sea: 1931–1932

1. The word he used was *mocoso*.

2. Bizkaian variation of *Euskalduna*.

3. Located at the mouth of the Guadalquivir River. The city of Seville is farther upriver.

Four. Alien in the Country: 1932

1. Urrutia said that the taxi took him to the Hotel Español, but he may be talking about a generic name by which Aguirre's Casa Vizcaina was known to the taxi drivers.

Five. Lonely Sheepherder: 1932–1936

1. "Guerry" was a short version of his Basque surname, too long for American ears. Urrutia is not totally sure if his first name was John.

2. Many sheepherders did not speak English, but most of them learned the swear words quickly.

3. Some of Urrutia's recollections are corroborated in Louise Shadduck, *Andy Little, Idaho Sheep King: An Anecdotal Biography of a Memorable Sheep Man* (Caldwell, Idaho: The Caxton Printers, Ltd., 1990), chapter 11.

Six. In Logging Camps: 1936–1940

1. He may have said "Basco," the term often used in Idaho. In the narrative, Urrutia uses Basco and Basque indiscriminately.

2. Bizkaian dialect for *nongoa haiz*.

Seven. California Beginnings: 1940–1944

1. Maria Urrutia's partner in the Boise boardinghouse.

2. They are all dead now. The eldest died in February 1999.

3. It would seem that Urrutia was not totally illegal, because in 1940 in Boise he was given some documents and allowed to go back to work.

4. Joseph Kreiss, "Mr. Idaho's Life Testament to U.S. Work Ethic," *Lassen County Times* (Susanville, California), 6 February 1996, 17A.

5. The word *criminal*, which sounds much the same in Basque or in Spanish, is reserved ordinarily for murderers. That is why he was so shocked.

6. In fact, he appears photographed with Urrutia and dozens of others when they volunteered for the army ca. 1942.

Eight. Working For Royal Grocery: 1944–1966

1. The *Lassen Advocate* (Susanville, California), 16 May 1980, 3.

2. After losing the war in 1878, Basques were forced to serve in the Spanish army, but many young men preferred to emigrate to the Americas rather than subject themselves to military service.

3. The newspaper says 1956.

4. He was no kin relationship to his wife.

Nine. Idaho Grocery: July 1, 1968

1. *Susanville* (California) *Lassen Advocate,* 16 May 1980, 1–3.

2. Ibid., 3.

3. Joseph Kreiss, "Mr. Idaho's Life Testament to U.S. Work Ethic," *Lassen County Times* (Susanville, California), 6 February 1996, 17A.

4. Ibid.

Ten. Visiting the Basque Country

1. About 150 *pesetas* = $1 in 1999.
2. The custom of *txikito*-drinking has diminished greatly during the week, but it picks up over the weekend. However, more beer is consumed than wine.
3. *Mus* is played somewhat like poker.
4. They don't have pool halls in the rural areas, but Galdakao is more urban than rural.
5. Franco was a fascist and ally of Hitler and Mussolini, and without their help the outcome of his rebellion against the elected republic would have been quite different.
6. Incidentally, the *New York Times* Sunday Travel Section (9 May 1999, 6, 18) featured a photograph and a review of Andra Mari Restaurant in Galdakao, Bizkaia.
7. Urrutia is talking about the Basque armed group ETA (*Euskadi Ta Askatasuna*, or Basque Country and Freedom), who from the late 1950s through the 1990s waged war against Franco and then against the Spanish state and police. There is little doubt that ETA was instrumental in the relative liberalization of Spain after Franco's death, and especially in the Basques obtaining home rule. In 1998 ETA announced an indefinite cease-fire.

Chapter Eleven. The Good Life in Susanville

1. Telephone conversation with Mary Jane, who lives in San Francisco, June 13, 1999.
2. Recently, in an article that appeared in a publication devoted to ranching, Robert Urrutia, "the Basque butcher," was quoted as saying that he "knows where his hamburger comes from." Ceci Dale-Cesmat, "Who Fed the Beef?" *Range Magazine* (Fall 1999):25.
3. Joseph Kreiss, "Farm Bureau: 'Mr. Idaho' Is Our Kind of Guy," *Lassen County Times* (Susanville, California), 19 November 1996, 5A.
4. Ibid.
5. Mr. Idaho today speaks a curious blend of several Basque dialects, but it is heavily tinted with his wife's brand of Basque from Esterenzubi in Iparralde, which is the one the children learned.
6. Urrutia remarked that, a few days later, his brother-in-law, too, died suddenly in Castro Urdiales, Cantabria, Spain, at seventy-six years of age.

1. For further information, see Gorka Aulestia, *Basque-English Dictionary* (Reno: University of Nevada Press, 1989), a19–a20.

2. With transitional verbs, *umeak* can also be ergative, meaning "child, the."

BASQUE PHONETICS AND GLOSSARY

Euskara Sounds and Their English Equivalents

Most of Euskara can be read like Spanish. Below are some relevant exceptions:

Euskara	English
h	*h* (as in *hot*, used in northern dialects)
s	*s* (as in *sea*)
tt	*no* correspondence, but similar to *t*
tx	*ch* (*atx* = *ach*, like *such*)
tz	the same
x	*sh* (*kaxa* = *casha*, like *cash*)
z	*ss* (is in *miss*)

Note that the *-a* at the end of many nouns is the article *the,* and the *-ak* denotes the plural form. Thus, *ume* = child; *umea* = child, the; *umeak* = children, the.

Aitita. Grandfather (*aitatxi* is also used)
Akulu. Spur, goad
Ama. Mother
Amatxi. Grandmother
Amuma. Grandmother
Arroza. Rice
Artogie. Corn bread (Bizkaian article often ends in *e*)
Artozopa. Corn and milk dish
Asto. Donkey
Aska. Trough
Auzo Eskola. Country schools built in remote hamlets
Azabu. A handful of tied-up wheat stalks

Bai. Yes
Baserri. Basque farmstead
Baserritar. Basque peasant
Bekelarri. Hamlet in Bizkaia where Urrutia was raised as an infant
Bixigu. Sea bream
Bizkaitar. Bizkaian; also, Basque nationalist

Erromeri. Country fiesta with folk dancing
Esne. Milk
Esnezopa. Bread and milk dish
Espartinak. Slippers
Etxekoandra. Lady of the House
Euskadi. Modern name for the Basque Country (according to
    today's political make-up, Euskadi comprises the Autonomous
    Region of Bizkaia, Gipuzkoa, and Araba)
Euskaldun. Basque-speaking person; a Basque
Euskal Herria. Basque Country (made up of six historical regions:
    Araba, Bizkaia, Gipuzkoa, Lapurdi, Nafarroa, and Zuberoa)
Euskara. Basque language
Ez. No

Galdakao. Town of Bizkaia where young Urrutia lived.
Garrafoi. Large, padded glass wine container
Gaueko. People of the night, according to Basque mythology

Hegoalde. Spanish Basque Country

Iparralde. French Basque Country
Ittaurren. Walking in front of the oxen to guide them when
    plowing.
Iturri. Spring, usually a developed one

Kalderea. Cauldron
Kale. Street
Kaletar. Urban people
Kaxak. Deep, large hardwood trunks for storage
Kinkileru. Door-to-door salesman in rural areas

Laratz. A heavy hook hanging down from the chimney
Lebatz. Hake

Mantxue. One-armed person
Maketo. Non-Basque, derogatory term
Marmitones. Spanish term for kitchen helpers on ships
Milesker denei. One thousand thanks to all
Mus. Popular Basque card game

Naboak. Stock beets; also called *arbi*

Ogi. Bread
Otto. Uncle

Para. A large steel spatula for baking sheepherder-type loaves of
   bread
Pentzu. Stock feed
Peseta. Spanish money

Sala. Formal living room
Sardinak. Sardines

Talo. Corn tortillas, Basque style
Tanta. Aunt
Txakolina. Green wine grown in the humid area of the Basque
   Country
Txapelak. Berets
Txikito. A shot of wine
Txipiroi. Calamari
Txorizo. Basque sausage

Zizare. Tapeworms
Zahagi. Large pigskin for storing wine